Broadway Christian Church Fort Wayne
A Love So Big
Walsh, Sheila

P9-AZV-779

0000   5071

A LOVE *SO* BIG

SHEILA WALSH

A LOVE

so BIG

ANCHORING YOUR CHILD TO THE HEART *of* GOD

=== *A Parent's Greatest Privilege* ===

WATERBROOK
PRESS

A LOVE *SO* BIG
PUBLISHED BY WATERBROOK PRESS
2375 Telstar Drive, Suite 160
Colorado Springs, Colorado 80920
A division of Random House, Inc.

Grateful acknowledgment is given to Henry Cloud and John Townsend for their insightful work in *Boundaries* (Grand Rapids: Zondervan, 1992), which is referenced in this book.

Details in some anecdotes and stories have been changed to protect the identities of the persons involved.

ISBN 1-57856-332-1

Published in association with the literary agency of Alive Communications, Inc., 7680 Goddard Street; Suite 200, Colorado Springs, CO 80920.

Library of Congress Cataloging-in-Publication Data
Walsh, Sheila, 1956–
   A love so big : anchoring your child to the heart of God / Sheila Walsh.—1st ed.
      p. cm.
   ISBN 1-57856-332-1
      1. God—Love. 2. Child rearing—Religious aspects—Christianity. 3. Children—Religious life.   I. Title.

BT140 .W35 2002
231'.6—dc21

                                                    2001046800

Printed in the United States of America
2002—First Edition

10 9 8 7 6 5 4 3 2 1

This book is dedicated with love to Mary Graham,
president of Women of Faith.
Mary, I am one of the millions whose lives have been eternally changed
by God's love poured through your life.

But thanks be to God, who always leads us
in triumphal procession in Christ
and through us spreads everywhere
the fragrance of the knowledge of him.

2 CORINTHIANS 2:14

══ CONTENTS ══

ACKNOWLEDGMENTS

To publisher Dan Rich and the entire WaterBrook Press team... Thank you for your encouragement and for your pursuit of excellence in all you do.

To Steve Arterburn... You are a brilliant man with a tender heart. Thank you for your partnership in Children of Faith. May God continue to give us new dreams together.

To Thelma Wells, Patsy Clairmont, Marilyn Meberg, Luci Swindoll, Barbara Johnson, Nicole Johnson, and Mary Graham... Women of Faith who love so big.

To those of you who have shared your lives and your stories with me... thank you.

To Traci Mullins... You are so much more than an editor. You are an encourager and friend. You take my words, you hear my heart, and you put all the pieces in place. Thank you!

To Barry and Christian... I love you.

A LOVE *SO* BIG

Arise, shine, for your light has come,
and the glory of the LORD rises upon you.

ISAIAH 60:1

I am not an expert on raising children. I have one child, and he is just four years old. The jury will be out for some time on how effectively my husband and I have communicated the love of God to our son and how fertile his heart is to receive that love and respond with openness.

During my pregnancy my daily prayer was "God, show me how to love my child in such a way that he will hunger to know you." I read everything available on how to be a model Christian parent. I dipped into both extremes, from those who propose a strong Old Testament–type discipline to those whose advice could have come from Alex Keaton's hippie parents on the television sitcom *Family Ties*. Both made convincing arguments supported by experience, documented results, and Scripture. Their positions were compelling—and diametrically opposed.

As a new parent, I found that overwhelming. It's one thing to make mistakes knitting a sweater, quite another rearing a child. It is so much easier to break a child than to repair one. So I was drawn again to one of my life verses: "If any of you lacks wisdom, he should ask God, who gives generously to all without finding fault, and it will be given to him" (James 1:5).

As I flipped through the pages of my life, I thought of peers who were raised in good, strong Christian homes and yet walked away from a personal faith. From my observations their environment appeared loving and kind, the faith of their parents tangible and credible. I thought of others whose parents would never be featured in *Parent of the Month* magazine, who professed no personal faith, and yet those children had fallen madly in love with Jesus. I looked for common threads. I looked for one consistent element I could emulate.

Of course it wasn't that simple, but there was something. I saw it in my own life. I saw it in the lives of others whose stories were very different from mine. What I found was that children who were raised by parents truly in love with Christ, who treasured their friendship with God above anything else, were more easily drawn to the heart of God. It wasn't that rules and discipline were absent; it was that they were not the point. They were the framing of the stage, not the central play itself. The real point was "God is beautiful. You are beautiful. God loves you on your good days and your bad days. There is nothing in this world that could make him stop loving you. God's love is *so* big it will never fade away."

A conversation I had one evening at the end of a Women of Faith conference drove this home for me. A woman in her seventies stood before me with tears streaming down her face. I held her for a moment until she was able to articulate what had moved her so deeply.

"I have been in church all my life," she explained. "I've been in Bible studies and home groups. I've tried so hard to live a good life, so hard. Tonight I finally understood for the first time: God loves me. It's as simple as that. He just loves me."

JESUS LOVES ME, THIS I KNOW

I thought about that woman a lot over the next few days. It had taken her an entire lifetime to grasp the amazing truth of God's immeasurable gift of love for her. I wondered how it would have affected the course of her life, how much joy and peace she would have enjoyed, if she had understood this simple but revolutionary message as a child. How would it have affected the lives of her children and grandchildren?

We will never experience that kind of outrageous, boundless, continuously flowing love in human flesh. Life is full of disappointments, silent wounds inflicted on our souls. I hear the cry from my son, from my husband, from myself: "That's not fair!" Life will never be fair, so what can we give our children that will anchor them to the heart of God in the midst of life that at times seems senseless and cruel?

We all long to be accepted, although we feel that at many levels we are not acceptable. The only place we will find that security and stability in an unaccepting world is in God. Not simply in the rules and regulations that make us "look" like believers but in God himself, in a passionate love relationship with him. That is why I gave my life to Christ as a young girl. I wanted to know the person who was so important to my mother. I wanted to know the One who comforted her and loved her, who gave her that quiet strength in the midst of her most difficult moments. I envied her relationship with Christ and wanted it for myself.

I know now that my mother struggled financially when my two siblings and I were little, but I didn't really understand then that we were poor. I knew I was the only girl who received free school meals because my father had died and my mother's only income was a widow's pension, but I had no sense of being deprived because of the peace and grace in my mother's life.

For those children who are raised in homes where there is no belief in God, his spectacular sovereignty in reaching out in other ways is silencing. God does not abandon. He finds ways through grandparents or the kindness of a schoolteacher or the parents of a friend to shine his light into the darkness of a soul without Christ. Some of the stories in this book pay tribute to that.

What do you do, however, if you have never received the love of God for yourself and now as a parent stand with an empty bowl? How do you pass on something you don't have? What do you do if you were never loved as a child and now struggle to pass on what you were denied?

I have watched families where there is sadness and abuse. The children seem to carry the weight of a world of which they should not even be aware. Perhaps you were raised in a home where there was little love to spare. You may have experienced abuse in the name of love, and now you are terrified you will pass on that legacy to your own children. Perhaps the religious instruction you received was cruel and heartless, cold and faceless. This book is for you, too. Through the following chapters we will take a fresh—perhaps for some a new—look at God's heart toward all his children, whether they are three or eighty-three.

OUR GREATEST PRIVILEGE

The wonderful fact is that no matter how much we love our children or others' children, God loves them more. At our best moments we are merely earthen vessels to contain his grace and truth. Children learn far more by what they observe than by what they are told. They are not an easy or a quick sale. They respond to truth and integrity before they can ever spell those words. Our challenge as parents and friends of young children is to live out our relationship with God in such reality and with such passion that we stir the same desire in them. It's our challenge to begin to comprehend the vast ocean of the love of God so that our children will know it will never run dry.

Beginning about age three, children acquire concepts and attitudes that form foundations that last a lifetime. We have all witnessed the simple yet transforming faith of a child. To nurture this powerful gift in our children is one of the most important missions we have on this earth. Out of my own passion for this mission, in 2000 I helped to establish an entertainment and production company called Children of Faith to minister to children. Our goal is to develop products that will positively impact children and their families around the world—to nurture in the vital formative years of children's lives a lasting connection between them and God and to keep them connected to their parents.

It is our hearts' desire through Children of Faith that God will speak loudly to little hearts and souls. It is also our hearts' desire to provide a channel through which God can speak to tired hearts and weary souls of all ages. Our passion is to provide the loving environment to produce a generation of children who "get it." We long to see the joy of children who understand that the God of the universe is crazy about them. Our prayer is to infuse the children entrusted to us from God with hearts to follow him and to lead lives that make him happy because they love him, not just because they've been told they have to or suffer the consequences.

There is no greater privilege in life than this. As a mother or father, there is no higher calling. As followers of Christ, it is our joyful mission to drink deeply of the love of God and pass it on. It is a love *so* big.

Love

Could we with ink the ocean fill,
And were the skies of parchment made,
Were every stalk on earth a quill,
And every man a scribe by trade,
To write the love of God above
Would drain the ocean dry.
Nor could the scroll contain the whole,
Though stretched from sky to sky.

O love of God, how rich and pure!
How measureless and strong!
It shall for evermore endure
The saints' and angels' song.

—Frederick M. Lehman, "The Love of God"

1

═ LOVE ═

AN UNFAMILIAR FACE

For I am convinced that neither death nor life, neither angels nor demons,
neither the present nor the future, nor any powers, neither height nor depth,
nor anything else in all creation, will be able to separate us
from the love of God that is in Christ Jesus our Lord.

ROMANS 8:38-39

The one thing we can never get enough of is love.
And the one thing we can never give enough of is love.

HENRY MILLER

I was shooting a music video at the beginning of 2001. The song was the old Welsh hymn "The Love of God." My husband, Barry, and I decided that it would be good to have our four-year-old son in the video. In retrospect I wonder why. (What do they say about working with animals and children?) But Christian was very excited.

"Will there be anyone else I know in the video?" he asked.

"Yes, I'll be in it," I said.

"I meant anyone famous like Batman or Spider-Man."

"No, I don't think they'll be in the video."

"Do I have to wear goofy clothes?"

I showed him the two suggested outfits, and they passed his cynical eye. His part was simple. All he had to ask me was, "Mommy, how much does God love me?"

The evening before the shoot Barry asked me to have several answers prepared for Christian, to give the producers a choice when they were editing the video. I sat staring at a blank sheet of paper for about an hour. When he came into my study later, he asked me what I had.

"I have a list," I said.

"Can I read it?"

"I don't think that will be necessary!" I replied.

"Please. I need to see what you have."

My list of answers to "How much does God love me?"

> A lot.
> Really a lot.
> Good grief, what a lot!
> More than you can imagine.
> With his whole heart.

"That's it?" Barry asked, eyeing bookshelves filled with Spurgeon's sermons, the writings of C. S. Lewis, Dostoevsky, and Solzhenitsyn.

"Well, how do you explain the love of God to a four-year-old child?" I asked.

"I don't know," he replied. "That's your job!" He was kidding…I think.

As I sat outside that night looking up at the stars, so breathtakingly beautiful in the winter air, I thought about my struggle for words. The depth of the love of God is so profound, so foreign to human experience, that the greatest hope we have to convey it to a child is to model it for them. And of course our best modeling will be so imperfect, limited, human.

The day of the video shoot arrived. Christian looked up at me, cameras rolling, and asked, "Mommy, how much does God love me?" I looked into his big brown eyes. It was such a simple scripted question from a four-year-old boy, but I saw a rare spiritual moment dropped into a vast array of questions such as, "Why doesn't the cat like balloons tied to her tail?" It's one of those moments parents look for to plant eternal seeds into the fertile soil of a child's curious mind. I wanted my answer to make sense to my son, to provoke future spiritual questions.

"God loves you so much, Christian. More than you could ever imagine." I silently rapped my own knuckles for providing such a vague and ethereal answer.

"This much?" he asked, stretching his arms as wide as he could.

"More," I responded.

"This much?" he asked, his face beet red with his wholehearted effort to make his arms stretch farther.

"Even more."

"Is God bigger than Spider-Man?"

"Well, yes. Plus, God is real, and Spider-Man is a cartoon," I said.

"That's not true, Mom. I met the real Spider-Man at Universal Studios. I've never met the real God."

Round one to Spider-Man. (That little exchange was edited out of the video!)

Why was it so hard for me to put into words for my child the depth of the love of God? Is it simply that the love of God is so profound that it eludes human description? Or is it that my "real," day-to-day world is so familiar and ever present that the spiritual realm takes a backseat in the dialogue of my mind, a deficit that is exposed when my son asks a straightforward question infused with eternal significance?

The more I thought about Christian's question, the more convinced I became that there is no more important question a child or an adult can ask, because the answer to that question is life changing; it is completely transforming.

TOO GOOD TO BE TRUE?

I thought again of the lady I mentioned in the introduction who had spent a lifetime in a religious fog, searching for what was right in front of her eyes. How is it possible to go to church all of your life and never understand the most simple, profound truth that the God of the universe loves you as you are, right now? Our churches and cathedrals are full of people just like this woman. I have been just like this woman. How sad to march in the parade of the faithful and not know the joy of festive song or even the reason we are marching. All that some of us know is we are very tired.

I wonder if this is the greatest deficit in our understanding of Christianity. We accept intellectually the theological truth that salvation is by faith alone, and yet we spend the rest of our lives trying to jump through hoops in the hope that God will love us more if we're "better." We reinforce that behavior in one another by our disapproval of each other and our Pharisaical judgments. At the age of forty-four, I am utterly convinced that there is nothing you or I can do to make God love us, and there is nothing we can do to stop his loving us. It has taken me a long time to come to that acceptance, and I still yearn to understand more deeply.

I constantly receive e-mails and notes from those who cannot begin to imagine that something that good could be true. I received a letter recently from a woman who told me some of the sad events and bad choices of her life. Anne's account of drug abuse, physical abuse, infidelity, rape, and abortion was harrowing to read. She is now living with her third husband, Steve, and they have rededicated their lives to Christ. But Anne is haunted by guilt and the remarks of some in her church who told her that if she really loved God, she would leave husband number three and try to find number one and remarry him.

"They tell me that God does not recognize my marriage to Steve, so he will not hear my prayers. But my first husband was a drunk who beat me. What should I do? I have never really known love in my life. I should have known this new life was too good to be true."

As I prayed for Anne and her husband and children, my heart ached for all of them. As I wrote to her, I wondered how often this kind of scenario is played out in our homes and churches.

If we could pass on the love of God, big and boundless and free, to our children, we would give them the greatest gift a parent could ever offer. But we have to be convinced of it ourselves first. I believe the greatest challenge we face as parents is reflected in this question: How can we live out before our children a passionate belief that the love of God is *so* big if in the quiet rooms of our own minds we're not sure of that love ourselves? It's not possible to pass on what we do not ourselves possess.

As I continued to pray for Anne and her family, I wondered how her children view God. Do they sense the judgment and weight of disapproval that she carries? When they sing "Jesus Loves Me, This I Know" in Sunday school, do they believe it?

WHAT DOES GOD LOOK LIKE?

I asked Christian one day what he thought God looked like.

"Big. Probably bigger than a tree," he said.

"Do you think he is kind?" I asked.

"I think so. He made our cat, Lilly, so that was sweet of him. Although I did ask him if he could turn me into Spider-Man, and that didn't happen."

"Where does he live?" I pursued.

"Up there," he answered, pointing to the sky. "Near the man on the moon."

Then it was his turn. "Mom, I love you more than God does!"

"Well, thank you, darling, but God loves us more than we could ever love each other."

"No way! I shared my marbles with you," he said.

"That's true, and that was very sweet of you. Do you know what God shared with us?" I asked.

"What?"

"His very own son, Jesus."

He thought about that for a moment. "I gave you two marbles."

Christian's child-questions leap out at unexpected moments. "Why can't I see God if he can see me?" "How can he live in your heart? That's gross! Is he tiny?"

How do I answer questions like that in a way that will make sense to a four-year-old with an active imagination and a nose that can sniff out uncertainty from four miles away? Our relationship with God is one of mystery and of questions with no easy answers. How do you rationally explain loving someone you can't see? How do you explain the mystery of prayer that makes room for the conundrum that at times you will ask God for something he is able to do and yet he will still say no? How do you explain death to a child?

Our son lost his paternal grandmother when he was two years old and his paternal grandfather when he was almost four. His questions at age two were different than they were at age four. We told him that Nana was no longer in her bed because she was living in heaven, so Christian went to put his shoes on, assuming we could visit. I told him that we couldn't do that right now, and he accepted it. When, two years later, he and I came home alone from the hospital emergency room, he said to me, "I hate this, Mommy. Why did God take my papa? I need him more than God does."

The day our son was born, the Record button was pushed. From that moment until the day he dies, his soul will record every moment. Some of the recordings will be at a conscious level and some at the sub-liminal level. The first three years of his life, pediatric experts say, set the foundation of many of his ideas, such as how he will form relationships, how he views himself and others, how he respects or disregards authority, and how through that framework he will then perceive God. I wonder…have Barry and I begun to give our son a picture of God that comes anywhere near reality?

A DAMAGED PICTURE

I think of my own childhood. If I may indulge in a little personal history here, you can perhaps see why I have struggled most of my life to believe that God's love is based solely on who he is and not on my performance.

I was born in a small town on the west coast of Scotland. My father was a traveling salesman, and my mother stayed home to raise three children. We attended a small church in the Scottish Brethren denomination, which was very strict, very conservative, and whose members at times, in my opinion, judged one another far more on outward appearance than on the condition of the heart.

My father had a severe car accident, which may have contributed to the blood clot that eventually lodged in his brain, causing a massive thrombosis. My brother was a baby at the time, I was three, and my sister was five. All we knew was that Daddy was in the hospital. We didn't understand any of the ramifications of the stroke, the permanent loss of speech, the paralysis on his left side.

After some time he came home. He was different. He never spoke again. A speech therapist came to the house to try to help him regain a basic vocabulary, but it was pointless. Whatever connection in the brain was necessary for her attempts to make sense to him was permanently severed.

I have very few memories of the next few months. I know from my mother that my dad's personality began to change, and he became violent at times. Eventually, after those incidents became severe and he turned his rage on me and on my mother, he was removed from our home. He died a few months later in a psychiatric hospital.

All I understood in the aftermath was that my dad was gone. I didn't attend a funeral or visit a gravesite; Daddy just never came home again. From that time until I was about eleven, I don't remember very much. My personality changed. I went from being a daredevil tomboy to being quiet and reserved, clinging to my mother for dear life.

However, I remember one night in 1967, when I was eleven years old, that eternally changed my life. An evangelistic music group from Edinburgh called The Heralds held a concert at our local cinema. Our family went. At the end of the evening, Ian Leitch, the evangelist, spoke for a few moments about the importance of a personal relationship with God. I remember his saying, "God has no grandchildren, only sons and daughters." He emphasized the necessity to choose to love God yourself; a personal relationship with Christ didn't happen by osmosis just because someone in your family believed. Several people went to the front of the theater that evening to be prayed for. I didn't. I was too shaken up by Leitch's message and convinced that my legs no longer had the power to move.

Later that night when I was at home in bed, the evangelist's words rang over and over in my head. Finally I went back downstairs and asked my mom if she would pray with me as I asked Jesus to come live in my heart and be my Savior forever. That night I became a Christian. I didn't understand very much, but I believed that God had heard my prayer and that he loved me. I will never forget that wonderful moment.

Unfortunately, my frame of reference for love, for relationship, for security was badly scarred by my experience with my dad, and I transferred those images to my heavenly Father. At some primal level I believed that no one is completely safe, no one loves you forever. I determined to be the perfect Christian. I was driven not simply to please God because he loved me and I loved him; rather, I wanted to make sure that he wouldn't stop loving me. I was convinced that my behavior influenced God's heart toward me, so I tried very hard to please him in every way.

I carried that distorted belief and damaged picture of God into my thirties. I was the classic "people pleaser." I didn't want to upset anyone or rock anyone's boat. I needed everyone to approve of me so I could approve of myself. That insatiable soul hunger propelled me through seminary, through years of traveling on the road with a contemporary Christian band, through five years as the co-host of *The 700 Club,* a daily religious talk show on the Christian Broadcasting Network. Everything came to a crashing halt in the fall of 1992 when I was finally—and, I believe, mercifully—diagnosed with clinical depression and admitted to a psychiatric hospital. I was terrified. My worst nightmare—that I would end up in a psychiatric hospital as my father had—became my reality. My "perfect Christian woman" mask lay shattered on the hospital's parking lot, and I had nothing to take its place but a haunted, tear-streaked face.

But God was at work. The place of my apparent undoing became the beginning of a new life for me.

> The Spirit of the Sovereign LORD is on me,
>> because the LORD has anointed me
>> to preach good news to the poor.
> He has sent me to bind up the brokenhearted,
>> to proclaim freedom for the captives
>> and release from darkness for the prisoners,
> to proclaim the year of the LORD's favor
>> and the day of vengeance of our God,
> to comfort all who mourn,
>> and provide for those who grieve in Zion—
> to bestow on them a crown of beauty
>> instead of ashes,
> the oil of gladness
>> instead of mourning,
> and a garment of praise
>> instead of a spirit of despair. (Isaiah 61:1-3)

That psalm became my song. I finally began to discover that God loves me because that is who he is—a God of love—not because of who I am or try to be. His love for me has nothing to do with my good performance or my poor performance. I am still unwrapping this wonderful gift. Its depths are fathomless.

TWISTED IDEAS ABOUT LOVE

How do you view God? Does he resemble someone in your personal history book? It's a worthwhile exercise to sit for a while and reflect on what the face of God looks like to you. You might be surprised by what you see. It's very difficult as adults to sort through the layer upon layer of ideas, emotions, experiences, and false beliefs that we have pasted onto our picture of God.

"He is like my father, demanding and difficult to please."

"He is like my mother, needy and manipulative."

"He is like my husband, cold and remote."

"He is like my wife, demeaning and cruel."

"He is like my boss, unfair and nepotistic."

"He is like everyone else who wants something from me."

Why would anyone want a relationship with someone like that? Why would we want to pass that on to our children?

Growing up on the west coast of Scotland, I was acutely aware of the warring factions in Northern Ireland. One of the saddest sights was to see small children throwing stones at British soldiers. Children don't know to hate. It is a learned behavior. And in Northern Ireland it is done in the name of God.

A few years ago I spent several days in Belfast, the capital of Northern Ireland. While there, I was delighted to be able to spend time with a group of Catholic priests and then have dinner with some local Protestant ministers. Both groups spoke in encouraging tones about what God was doing in Northern Ireland. When I asked if there would ever be an opportunity for them to meet together, to represent the love of God that is greater than all that divides them, my suggestion was greeted with great disdain. The Protestant ministers told me that if the Catholic priests were serious about God, they would leave the Roman Church and come over to their side. I understand that there are great theological disparities, but if the compelling love of God does not call us to put down our stones and reach out our hands, then how can we say we love the God of light and love?

> This is the message we have heard from him and declare to you:
> God is light; in him there is no darkness at all. If we claim to
> have fellowship with him yet walk in the darkness, we lie and do
> not live by the truth. But if we walk in the light, as he is in the
> light, we have fellowship with one another, and the blood of
> Jesus, his Son, purifies us from all sin. (1 John 1:5-7)

One of my favorite choruses from childhood Sunday school classes is

> Jesus loves the little children,
> All the children of the world.
> Red and yellow, black and white
> They are precious in His sight—
> Jesus loves the little children of the world.

When I married my husband, who is from Charleston, South Carolina, I realized that those simple lyrics had a controversial ring to his parents.

"We're not prejudiced," Barry's mother told me. "We had a colored gardener, and he had his own plate and mug."

I sat and stared at my mother-in-law in disbelief. I had no idea what to say. My husband looked at my face and shook his head.

"You have no idea what it was like to be raised in the South when my parents were young, Sheila," Barry said to me later. "It was a different time."

"Perhaps so, but how can someone claim to love God and look down on any group of people? I can't even begin to relate to that."

The backwash of my indignation left a lot of trash on my own shore, however. I thought of my personal list of the disenfranchised. I have a loathing for those who are judgmental. I stand in judgment of them! I thought then of the countless other groups of people that are marginalized in the name of God.

The homosexual community.

Those with AIDS.

The divorced.

Single people.

The sick.

The list continues, depending on where we were raised and what we personally despise. The only cure for our prejudice and hate is a baptism into the love of God that washes our eyes over and over till we see nothing but the love of God.

I realize this seems like heresy to some.

"If we reach out in love, we condone their sin!"

"To fellowship with people like that is a bad witness. It makes it seem as if their behavior is all right."

But what we pass on to our children through that kind of stance is that there is an A list and a B list when it comes to love. Those on the A list are people like us—those who live like us and love like us. The B list is everyone else.

That is not how Christ lived in human flesh, and he was very offensive to some. "While Jesus was having dinner at Matthew's house, many tax collectors and 'sinners' came and ate with him and his disciples. When the Pharisees saw this, they asked his disciples, 'Why does your teacher eat with tax collectors and "sinners"?'" (Matthew 9:10-11).

I think this has always been our greatest failure: We do not even begin to love as Jesus did. Even as we judge others, the bell tolls for us, too.

"If only I could lose weight, I would feel more like an overcomer."

(Unspoken line: *God would love me more.*)

"If I could just stay away from online pornography, I would feel more worthy of my wife's love."

(Unspoken line: *God would love me more.*)

"If only I could do something with this temper."

(Unspoken line: *God would love me more.*)

"If I, if I, if I…"

(Unspoken line: *God would love me more.*)

The specifics are different, but the gulf between our hungry soul and God's perfect love is the same.

In *Lake Wobegon Days,* Garrison Keillor tells a story of a man who returns to the small Minnesota town of his youth one Halloween night with a very particular mission in mind. In a Martin Luther "Wittenberg moment" he intends to nail a list of ninety-six offenses to the door of the Lutheran church he and his parents had attended. Many of the charges are against his parents and his upbringing in general. Some of the offenses are hilarious, as he describes the kind of food served to him, which, in retrospect, he thinks of more as ballast than nutrition. But as the list goes on, it becomes more poignant and devastating. He reflects on the way his parents deflected any compliment sent his way out of a compulsion to keep him humble, until their deflection was weightier than the kind words that had been spoken. His indictment of their staunch religious way of life is that all joy was squeezed out of his soul. He grew up thinking that God was like his parents. If he made one wrong move, he would be slapped down.

"You ask me why I don't call," he wrote. "I don't need to. Your voice rings in my head every day."

THE BLESSED AND THE UNBLESSED

Perhaps that was the experience of your childhood. You have worked hard, achieved, produced, but it's never enough. All you hear in your head is the disapproval that was served as regularly as milk. It is what author Karl Olsson describes in his book *Come to the Party* as the dilemma of the blessed and the unblessed.

In this honest and beautiful book, Olsson describes a lifetime of service to God that was like a millstone around his neck. As a child he never sensed his father's approval and spent the rest of his life trying to earn it in service for God, with little or no joy. He completed his graduate degree and doctorate in theology, ultimately becoming president of the seminary that served his denomination. He describes the way he punished himself, ruthlessly running himself into the ground in God's service in an attempt to quiet the internal voice that told him it was not enough.

Our churches are full of people who are overinvolved, up to their ears, and sick at heart, doing the "right thing." As with the story of the prodigal son, there is a party going on, but many are not going in. See if you can find yourself in this list of four categories Olsson provides of the blessed and the unblessed.

1. Those who doubt there is a party.
2. Those who believe there is a party somewhere but they are not invited.
3. Those who believe there is a party and they're invited but they don't deserve to stay.
4. Those who are invited and go and stay.

For a long time I was in the first category. My twisted view of God's love was that if you really wanted to please God, you would be miserable down here and happy in heaven. The thought of a party would have seemed flippant and worldly. But God broke into my dirge and began to play a different song.

That melody is what I want to pass on to my son. I want him to know he is loved, he is valued, God is on his side, he doesn't have to perform tricks or jump through hoops while the party ice cream melts. He's welcome to just come to the table!

Perhaps like the bitter, disillusioned man who returned to Lake Wobegon, who even in his moment of truth left his note unsigned, you carry in your heart and head every negative thing you were ever told about yourself and the world.

"You can't trust anyone but yourself!"

"You can do better than that!"

"Oh, don't bother, I'll do it myself!"

"You're always like that. You'll never change!"

"Are you going to eat all that? I thought you were on a diet."

"I wish you'd never been born."

The voices that ring in our heads are far worse than a momentary insult or hurt because we carry them everywhere we go. We may be able to put distance between ourselves and the ones who shot the arrows, but their words still have a backstage pass to our souls.

Sometimes when I'm channel surfing, I stop on a daytime talk show. I have a morbid fascination with the public bloodletting that takes place in the impersonal setting of a television studio. It is indicative of the people we have become that we find it easier to reveal our secrets to a million people rather than to just one. One person would hold us accountable. A million strangers cannot. It becomes obscene, however, when children are introduced in the midst of screaming adults and parents. The pain and confusion written on their faces is heartbreaking. How will these children grow up with any sense of self-respect or security? When they hear of the love of God, what do they see in their minds?

"MOMMY, HOW MUCH DOES GOD LOVE ME?"

I love books. I collect them like pieces of fine china and display them in my office—row upon row of mysteries waiting to be unwrapped, full of gifts and surprises. I had a healthy collection of children's books before Christian came along and have added to it since. I believe that a good children's book has layer upon layer of meaning that keeps unfolding through the years, and I look for new books that fit that criteria.

I recently came across a book by R. C. Sproul, *The Priest with Dirty Clothes,* which I gladly added to my collection. The jacket said that it was for six- to ten-year-olds. It was sitting on my chair in the lounge one evening, and Christian picked it up.

"Read me this one, Mommy."

"This might be too old for you," I said.

He looked at me as if he were Miss Tennessee and I had just told her that she couldn't use hair spray. I started to read. Barry came and sat down by the fire as I read on.

The story begins in Scotland with a grandfather telling his two grandchildren a story about the love of God. The tried-and-true method of parable works beautifully here. In short, the priest in the story wants to deliver his first sermon to the king, but his clothes are filthy, and he can't get the dirt off. He meets a prince, who exchanges his spotless robes for the priest's filthy ones. Now the priest is fit to appear before the king. He wears those new robes for the rest of his life.

"What did you think of the story?" I asked Christian.

"I liked it," he said.

"What part did you like best?"

"I liked the prince."

"Why?"

"He was kind, and he didn't mind having mud on his clothes."

In simple form that is God's story. He is unspeakably kind and gladly took the mud of our lives upon himself. He took all the mud, not just your mud or my mud—all the mud. A painful history in our personal relationships can be a barrier to understanding the love of God, but the very nature of the love of God can be a barrier in itself. God's very kindness, his acceptance of all sorts of mud, can be a barrier to our relinquishing ourselves to his love. Why? Because most of us have a list of the unlovable and unforgivable etched into our souls.

Ask Anne. She will tell you what that list sounds like in her church. I don't believe it's possible to fully receive the truth that God loves me if I do not in the same moment believe that God also loves you. So often we despise what we are afraid of becoming. Evangelist Jimmy Swaggart spoke out passionately about sexual impropriety, seeing in others the sins that pulled at him. He is a familiar example, but our churches, our homes, and our hearts are full of them. We pass on our petty preferences to our children and then wonder why they resist the love of God that is so much bigger than our tiny hearts.

The love of God is not an add-on to our faith. It is everything. It transforms everything. God's love did not propel him to send Christ to the cross so that we could try to be like him but so that he would live in us. I'd like to repeat that. *God's love did not propel him to send Christ to the cross so that we could try to be like him but so that he would live in us.* We can't be like God! God is perfect. God is pure and spotless. What we can do is invite God to live in and through us. He is the only hope we have.

A dear counselor friend of mine, Dr. Gripka, told me that Christ has not come to get me out of tough situations but to *live in me through them.* Do you see the difference? It's not about our trying hard to be better but our relinquishing ourselves to the love of God and letting him flow through us to others. God's love makes everything new. It takes our old lists and nails them to the cross until the spilling blood has made them illegible.

Every night before I tuck my son into bed, we have a little ritual: We tell each other what we are grateful for. Sometimes his list is as simple as "I'm grateful that the cat didn't throw up in my room today." At times, it is more profound. "I'm so glad you love me. I'm glad Daddy loves me. I'm glad God is bigger than the bogeyman."

Whatever else we include or miss depends on how tired he is or I am, but I never forget this part: "Remember, darling, whether you make good choices or bad choices, God loves you and so do we. Whether you are naughty or nice, God loves you and so do we. God always, always loves you. If there were twenty million four-year-old boys in the world and I could be a mommy to any of them, I would still choose you."

Christian smiles, curls up on his side, and closes his eyes. I often sit and watch him sleep. I find myself wishing I could protect him from all the things and people that will harm him, but I know I can't. In those moments my most fervent prayer is that his understanding and experience of the love of God will be as deep as the marrow in his bones. I believe that if he knows God loves him with a vast and everlasting love, then Barry and I will have done the job entrusted to us.

I have lived through the death of parents; I have watched and wept with friends over the death of a child. Somehow we survive those blows, wounded, bleeding, but still walking. But how can we survive without the love of God? If we are without that, we live with no pattern to the mass of threads that make up our lives. If you find yourself in the list of those outside the range of streamers and balloons, I pray that you will open your heart to the love song of God that invites you to the party. It's never too late to show up. There is no dress code; you just come.

That is what the gospel of good news is all about: God is kind and didn't mind getting mud on himself so you and I could have a place at the table. Danish philosopher Søren Kierkegaard wrote, "When Christ cried, 'My God, my God, why have you forsaken me?' it was a terrible moment for Christ. But, I believe, that it was more terrible for God to hear his cry."

God went to extremes too terrible to contemplate to answer Christian's question, "Mommy, how much does God love me?"

With everything he is, with all his blood and all his tears.

"Mommy, how much does God love me?"

Christ stretched out his arms on a cross of wood and said, "This much!"

"How big is God's love?"

Christ stretched out his arms on a cross of wood and said, "This big!"

"Greater love has no one than this, that he lay down his life for his friends" (John 15:13).

Grace

May the grace of Christ our Saviour
And the Father's boundless love,
With the Holy Spirit's favor,
Rest upon us from above.
Thus may we abide in union
With each other and the Lord,
And possess, in sweet communion,
Joys which earth cannot afford.

—John Newton, "May the Grace of Christ
Our Saviour"

2

$=$ GRACE $=$

LOVE WITH OUTSTRETCHED ARMS

*Therefore, since we have been justified through faith, we have peace
with God through our Lord Jesus Christ, through whom we have
gained access by faith into this grace in which we now stand.*

ROMANS 5:1-2

*If Garp could have been granted one vast and naive wish,
it would have been that he could have made the world safe for children.*

JOHN IRVING

The hardest job I've ever had is being a mother. I became pregnant at
forty, and as I have since joked with my friends, I now realize I
should have slept more the first forty years! My mother and sister
tried to prepare me for the wonder and trauma of actually giving
birth, but I was deaf to their well-meaning words.

"I can do this. I've been to the dentist. I've had things out before!"

My doctor scheduled the delivery, a job once looked upon as God's,
for the fourteenth of December. She explained to me that she was going
on vacation to New York and if I wanted her to deliver, she would
induce. I told her I could wait. By my thirty-second week, I had decided
not to give birth until I was really ready, which I estimated to be in
about two more years. She was adamant. I was clueless, so she arranged
for me to come into her office, which as it turned out was mercifully

near the hospital, on the twelfth, thirteenth, and fourteenth. I was given some kind of gel, which was supposed to make the whole party kick in smoothly by the afternoon of the fourteenth.

I made it home on the twelfth, feeling as if I had just been given enough dynamite to shoot my poor son to the moon. Barry and I returned the next day for the same procedure. When it was over, the nurse said, "Now, just walk around a little, dear, before you go home."

As soon as my feet hit the floor, I knew I was about to give birth to my son, an elephant, and every internal organ in my body. The nurse rushed me over to the hospital and told me I had gone into labor too fast. I tried to explain that this was not my idea, only to discover that women who are about to give birth think they are talking, but apparently nothing is coming out of their mouths, because everyone in the room ignores them. I had told Barry I didn't want anyone but him in the delivery room, but when the curtain went up on the main event, I would gladly have accepted help from the pizza delivery guy.

Christian was born on the thirteenth, and on the fourteenth we went home. I couldn't believe they were expecting me to hobble home with this tiny bundle who was just a few hours old. I said to the nurse, "Couldn't I just stay for a couple of weeks until I get the hang of this?" She left the room laughing. I never saw her again.

Barry has very fond memories of the first three months. I have very few. I was in pain, exhausted, and overwhelmed. We had a large golden retriever, and I was convinced the dog was going to sit on the baby or worse. Memories of Meryl Streep running through the bush shouting, "The dingo got my baby, the dingo got my baby!" flooded over me about three o'clock every morning.

Then Christian smiled. It was a profound moment for me. I know that he probably just had gas, but when he smiled at me, I heard him say, "It's okay, Mom. You're doing fine. This is going to be great!"

The first two years of Christian's life were physically hard for me as I dealt with the sleepless nights and the need to keep an eagle eye on him as soon as he could crawl. (He was able to crawl at the speed of a BMW but with more noxious emissions.) Those years were also filled with pure, unadulterated joy. In those early days his daddy and I were able to protect him from most things, but then the gates of his world began to open a little wider, and now being a mommy is hard in more ways.

I watch Christian from the car after I've dropped him off at Toddler Time at our church. I see him approach one boy he wants to play with, but that boy wants to play with someone else. I remember that feeling. Sometimes I still have it. I hear his cry as he falls off his bike and skins his knee. Barry and I sit and talk with him after he has been disciplined for disobedience, and big tears roll down his cheeks as he says, "I don't want to be disobedient." I understand that feeling too. I had forgotten how hard it is to be a child.

My prayer for my son, for me, for you is that our hearts will be filled with the love of God, which is the one big constant in an inconsistent world, and that we would know the grace of God—love with outstretched arms. Grace makes living in this world possible.

LIFE IS NOT FAIR

One of my pet phrases when I was a child was "That's not fair!" I remember one occasion when I was about ten years old and my brother, Stephen, was seven. I had a bad habit of sliding down the banister, trailing my shoe buckles behind me and leaving little track marks in the white paint. My mom, having had the banister repainted one more time, told me that if I did it again, I would be punished. I looked at the fresh, dry paint. I looked at the beautiful smooth surface of the banister that called to me like fresh snow to an ardent skier. I got on and took off. Halfway down I thought, *It might have been a good idea to take my sandals off.*

It was too late. I looked in horror at the ribbon of fresh paint standing up and saluting like a demented general. Just then I heard my brother's voice behind me: "I'm going to tell Mom!"

"No, don't! Please don't tell Mom," I cried, temporarily oblivious to the fact that it was fairly likely my mom would notice my disobedience anyway. I guess I was trying to buy myself some time.

Stephen replied, "I won't tell if you give me that bag of candy you're saving for the movie."

I was in a tough place. I had been waiting for two weeks to see *Cinderella* on television and had saved up my allowance to purchase a big bag of my favorite candy to eat while I watched. What to do? Finally I gave in. I handed over my bag, as precious to me as life savings.

My little brother sat down on the stairs beside me and ate the whole bag. Then to make it the crime of the century, he went and told my mom anyway! I was furious! I wanted my mom to disown him and send him to live with a man-eating tribe in the darkest jungle on the most distant continent with the largest snakes. Stephen was sent to his room for tattling, and I was sent to mine for disobedience.

When Mom came in to see me, she spanked me on my sit-upon for what I had done and for trying to enlist my brother to conceal my crime. She told me that I couldn't watch *Cinderella*. I was devastated. I was sad that I couldn't watch the movie, but I was more upset that I had gone directly against my mom's instructions and had disappointed her.

A short while later I heard a little knock on my bedroom door. It was my brother. "Go away," I said.

"Please let me come in," he answered. "I'm really sorry." He came in, and I could see that he was sorry for his part in the whole disaster.

"It was my own fault, Stephen. I forgive you. I should know better." He left. He seemed to be feeling a little sick.

I nodded off as I lay in exile, and when I woke, my mom was sitting on the end of my bed watching me.

"Mom, I am so sorry," I said. "I knew what I was doing was wrong, and I did it anyway. Then I pulled Stephen into it. I'm a bad, bad person."

My mother smiled at my familiar melodramatic ways. "You are not a bad person, Sheila. You just made a bad choice."

She dried my eyes and took me downstairs to watch *Cinderella!*

For me it was a moment of pure grace. I deserved everything she had measured out to me. I didn't deserve to see the movie, but her love for me stretched out its arms as grace—unmerited favor. Grace throws a rope to us and pulls us out of the dark places we have chosen and the dark places we did not choose.

Perhaps that is why we find grace so risky. "If someone's choice has landed her in a dark hole," we reason, "we shouldn't mess with that. To offer help would be to remove the consequence of sin." God forbid!

WHAT IS GRACE?

I was having my nails done in a mall somewhere in the Midwest in the spring of 2000. The technician asked me why we were in town. I told her we were having a Women of Faith conference there that weekend, and she asked what we were talking about. I said the conference's theme was "Extravagant Grace." She thought for a few moments and then said, "Do you mean, should we say it at meals or not?"

I understood her confusion. Grace is not a familiar word or concept to many people. We say that people are gracious, meaning they were kind and welcoming, but the radical type of grace the Bible talks about is a mystery to most of us.

Webster states one definition as "unmerited divine assistance given man for his regeneration or sanctification." Lewis Smedes, in his marvelous book *Shame and Grace,* says that "grace gives us the courage to look at the messy mixture of shadow and light inside of our lives." If we're honest, we must admit that we're a mixture of shadow and light.

God's grace, however, calls us to extremes far beyond our limited human logic.

Jesus told a story that illustrates the powerful ramifications of the calling of grace. We know it as the story of the Good Samaritan, and it is recorded in Luke 10:30-37. This story is the gospel of grace in a nutshell. I've known it since I was a child in Sunday school. It's a story we tell children, hoping they will learn to be nice to everyone, not just to those who are like them. The story is far more profound and disturbing than that, however, as it illustrates the extreme commitment and far-reaching consequences of grace as Jesus taught it.

The hatred between Jew and Samaritan was deep and had a long and bitter history. It is recorded on several occasions in the Old Testament. When the prophet Nehemiah was called to rebuild the walls of Jerusalem more than four hundred years before the birth of Christ, Sanballat, a very influential Samaritan who tried unsuccessfully to defeat Nehemiah's plans for rebuilding, tormented him. "He ridiculed the Jews, and in the presence of his associates and the army of Samaria, he said, 'What are those feeble Jews doing?'" (Nehemiah 4:1-2).

When Christ's accusers were attempting to discredit him, they said, "Aren't we right in saying that you are a Samaritan and demon-possessed?" (John 8:48). I'm not sure which label they considered to be the bigger insult!

Christ's encounter with the woman at the well is another example of the fact that both sides, Jew and Samaritan, knew there was a wall of hatred between them. "The Samaritan woman said to him, 'You are a Jew and I am a Samaritan woman. How can you ask me for a drink?' (For Jews do not associate with Samaritans.)" (John 4:9).

For Christ to choose a Samaritan to be the hero of the story recorded in Luke 10 must have sent his audience reeling.

The story of the Good Samaritan begins with a Jew who has been robbed, beaten, and left to die. The terrain would be familiar to Jesus' listeners. The distance from Jerusalem to Jericho is about seventeen miles, descending sharply toward the Jordan River just north of the Dead Sea. It was rugged, rocky land where robbers could easily hide. It was considered especially dangerous.

The first two men to see the man who lay by the side of the road were a priest and a Levite. Many priests lived in Jericho, so it would be common to see them traveling back and forth between their homes and Jerusalem. Priests served in the temple; their highest duty was to offer sacrifices. Levites assisted them in the maintenance of the temple services and order. Both priests and Levites were active in the service of God, called to acts of mercy and kindness, and yet they did nothing to help the Jew lying by the side of the road. They even crossed the street to avoid any possible contact with the wounded man.

Then a Samaritan came along. Every word that Christ uses to describe him is weighty. "When he saw the man's condition, his heart went out to him. He gave him first aid, disinfecting and bandaging his wounds. Then he lifted him on to his donkey, led him to an inn, and made him comfortable. In the morning he took out two silver coins and gave them to the innkeeper, saying, 'Take good care of him. If it costs any more, put it on my bill—I'll pay you on my way back'" (Luke 10:33-35, MSG).

The fact that the Samaritan took pity on the Jewish man is amazing in itself. It stands in stark contrast not only to the attitude of the priest and the Levite but also to the usual feelings of hostility between Jew and Samaritan. His pity moved him to sacrificial action. The Samaritan probably used pieces of his own clothing to make the bandages and his own wine as a disinfectant and his own oil as a soothing lotion. He put the man on his own donkey and paid the innkeeper out of his own pocket, with a promise to pay more if needed when he returned that way. He did everything that someone who professes to love God should have done.

Jesus told this story in response to a question from a scholarly man, a lawyer, who was familiar with God's law. "On one occasion an expert in the law stood up to test Jesus. 'Teacher,' he asked, 'what must I do to inherit eternal life?'" (Luke 10:25). Jesus asked him what is written in God's law. The man replied, quoting Deuteronomy 6:4-5, "Hear, O Israel: The LORD our God, the LORD is one. Love the LORD your God with all your heart and with all your soul and with all your strength." He knew the law well for he added, "Do not seek revenge or bear a grudge against one of your people, but love your neighbor as yourself" (Leviticus 19:18). Jesus told him he had answered well, and if he would do these things, he would inherit eternal life. It's not clear whether the lawyer asked his next question, "Who is my neighbor?" out of embarrassment at failing to trap Christ or as a genuine question, but his response at the end of the story reveals a lot about his heart.

When Christ finished telling the story, he asked this scholar which of the three men in the story acted in a loving way, as a "neighbor." The lawyer replied, "The one who had mercy on him." He couldn't even bring himself to say "the Samaritan." To a Jew, there was no such thing as a "good" Samaritan. But Christ used the Samaritan as the lawyer's teacher when he said, "Go and do the same." The implication is clear: If you ever see anyone in need of help, even if it is a Samaritan, get off your high horse, take your own stuff, and love him back to life. What a well-aimed insult for this lawyer. He had spent his whole life learning the law, and Jesus told him that he had missed the point!

As Meister Eckhart, who believed that the whole goal of the spiritual life is compassion, wrote, "If you were in an ecstasy as deep as that of St. Paul and there was a sick man in need of a cup of soup, it were better for you that you returned from the ecstasy and brought the cup of soup for love's sake." Meister Eckhart was a Dominican mystic who fell into the bad graces of the Roman Catholic Church but is viewed by many as a precursor to Martin Luther in his statements regarding being justified by faith alone. It seems it has never been popular to assert there is nothing we can do to win the love of God; it is a gift...of grace.

GRACE AND SHAME

One of the most damaging things we can do to our children is to shame them, to make them feel as if they have to hide who they really are. There are many ways to shame a child. Words are more damaging than bullets because the wounds sometimes never heal.

"How can you be so stupid?"

"You'll never be any different!"

"Her sister has the looks!"

We can shame with our body language. We need touch. We were born to be held and loved. The medical and psychological communities provide alarming statistics that show the devastation to children who are not held and loved. They don't grow and thrive. They are stunted physically and emotionally. I am continually amazed when I hear how little time many parents spend actually talking to their children each day. The latest research I read about reported that the average is seven minutes! No wonder so many children are powder kegs. They have no place to dump the daily hurts and indignities of life. They have been emotionally disowned by those closest to them, and as they grow, they disown themselves. Shame makes a child feel unworthy, unlovable, ugly inside and out. Many young girls become sexually promiscuous because they have no concept of being worth more. Grace can change all of that.

Let's stop here for a moment and consider what that would look like in our homes. Your daughter comes home from college and tells you with tears and terror in her eyes that she is pregnant. What does grace look like there? You discover questionable magazines under your son's bed. What does grace look like there? You catch your young child in a lie. What does grace look like there? The weighty dilemma for us as parents is to balance our calling from God to discipline our children in a culture that no longer honors that with our calling to love them and extend grace to them just as we have been loved and had grace extended to us by God.

I watched an episode of the *Montel Williams* talk show on the subject of discipline in June of 2001. There was a heated discussion between a police officer and the author of a book advocating love and grace in place of any form of discipline. The author's position was that the job of the police has become impossible because children no longer fear the consequences of their actions.

In listening to the two passionate points of view, my heart resonated more with the police officer's than the author's. Grace loses its weight if the consequences for sin are not felt. Grace is no lightweight gift. It is a get-out-of-jail pass written in the very blood of the Lamb of God. So how do we balance the two callings—to discipline our children and to show them grace with outstretched arms?

When my father-in-law first came to live with us, Christian said something that cut tender-hearted William to the core. Christian was upset about something, and he said to his papa, "Why don't you go home now? This is our house."

The look in William's eyes was heartbreaking. I sent Christian to his room.

"You know he doesn't mean that, Pop," I said.

"I know, I know," he replied. I knew he was hurt.

I went upstairs to talk to Christian. "I am very angry with you. You hurt your papa's feelings," I said.

Big tears began to run down his cheeks. "I'm sorry, Mommy."

"I'm glad you're sorry, but that's not enough," I said. "I want you to sit here for a while and think about what you said. Then I want you to go downstairs and ask Papa to forgive you. There will be no videos today."

A few minutes later he came downstairs. "I'm sorry, Papa!" he said, giving William a big hug.

"That's okay, boy," William said as he hugged him back.

Later that evening Christian wanted to watch one of his videos. I said no.

"But, Mommy, I said I was sorry, and Papa forgave me!"

"I understand that, darling, but there is a price to pay when we do the wrong thing."

He turned to a softer rock. "Papa, can I watch my video?"

"Sure!" William said, looking beseechingly at me.

"Papa said I can," my son announced with triumph in his voice.

"Christian, I don't care if you have a letter from the president of the United States of America. Tonight there will be no videos."

He thought about that for a bit. "And tomorrow?" he asked.

"Tomorrow is a whole new day!" I told him.

That's what is so wonderful about grace. It provides a place for us to face the consequences of our sin but not be destroyed by it. Tomorrow is a whole new day.

ROCKS

Nicole Johnson, author and dramatist, performs a sketch called "Rocks," which is now available in book form, *Dropping Your Rock,* at freshbrewedlife.com. It centers on the story told in John 8 of the woman caught in adultery and dragged before Christ to be stoned for her sin. Old Testament law stated the punishment clearly. "If a man commits adultery with another man's wife—with the wife of his neighbor—both the adulterer and the adulteress must be put to death" (Leviticus 20:10).

The religious leaders were determined to trap Christ. Would he disregard the law and therefore be liable to condemnation himself, or would he uphold it and lose his legacy of compassion before the people?

Jesus stooped down and began to write in the sand. This is the only record we have of Christ's writing. We don't know what he wrote, but as they continued to badger and question him, Jesus stood up and threw the decision back to the legalists. "If any one of you is without sin, let him be the first to throw a stone at her."

He continued to write in the sand. One by one, starting with the eldest, the people around Christ and the adulterous woman began to disperse, the dull thud of rocks sounding behind them. Finally they were all gone.

Can you imagine what it must have been like to be that woman? Notice that she had been dragged there alone. There was no man to share the weight of her punishment. It had been a trap, a setup, and she was the shamed and expendable one.

As Nicole points out in her sketch, there is something cathartic about stone throwing. We feel as if we are doing our part to rid the world of evil. As Christians it is easy to confuse a love for righteousness with a love of self-righteousness. I think of the stones I have thrown in my life, and I am ashamed. I threw stones toward those who tentatively confided a sin that was destroying them, and instead of comfort they received the sharp edge of a rock. If I could sit down with the thirty-year-old Sheila Walsh and talk to her about some of those actions, I know what she would say.

"But we can't condone sin."

"If I didn't tell her that what she was doing was wrong, then who would?"

"I'm pulling away from her to make her accountable for her actions."

It would be easy to find an "Amen!" for those statements in many circles. But Jesus simply gave the one with no darkness in his own heart the privilege of throwing the first stone. Slowly everyone walked away, the eldest first. There is something interesting in that, too. Perhaps we are more judgmental when we are young, more reluctant to extend grace, more determined to eradicate sin in others, hoping to exorcise our own private demons. What the woman heard as she cowered in the sand was the thud of grace as everyone's rocks fell to the ground. Jesus told her that he didn't accuse her but to go and sin no more.

What a gift to a woman whose life had been judged worthless!

Christ accepted her exactly where she was, forgave her, and saw in her the possibility for change. In his masterly work *City of God*, Augustine says that a friend is someone who knows everything there is to know about you and accepts you totally. Jesus said, "I have called you friends" (John 15:15).

This grace, this love with outstretched arms, is not only a New Testament doctrine. Think of the story of Jacob. He was a man who deceived his father and cheated his brother out of his inheritance and blessing. He came out of his mother's womb grasping at Esau's heel and never stopped.

To receive Isaac's blessing was not a small thing. "May nations serve you and peoples bow down to you. Be lord over your brothers, and may the sons of your mother bow down to you. May those who curse you be cursed and those who bless you be blessed" (Genesis 27:29). When Esau discovered what had happened, he was incensed and determined to kill Jacob, so Jacob ran away.

Stopping to rest for the night in a place called Bethel, Jacob had a theophany, an encounter with the living God. In a dream Jacob saw angels ascending and descending a stairway to heaven. At the top was Jehovah. God could have struck down Jacob as a deceiver and a cheat, but instead he blessed him. Jacob woke with his rock still by his side, a rock he'd picked up to ward off attack, whether from a wild animal or from his brother sneaking up on him in the night. Jacob took his rock and built an altar.

That would seem to be the thing to do with rocks when we taste grace: Build with them an altar to the honor and glory of a God who sees us asleep and vulnerable in our sin and rebellion, and instead of striking us down, he blesses us. The psalmist expressed it beautifully when he said, "If I say, 'Surely the darkness will hide me and the light become night around me,' even the darkness will not be dark to you; the night will shine like the day, for darkness is as light to you" (Psalm 139:11-12). God sees through the physical dark to find us and reaches through the darkness in our own souls to smile upon us with grace. God looks at his creation and calls us good! In her book *Amazing Grace,* Kathleen Norris says, "I suspect that only God and well-loved infants can see this way."

THE POISON OF UN-GRACE

Perhaps unwillingness to extend grace to others comes out of a deficit in our own lives. Perhaps we never felt like a well-loved infant and are still screaming inside, "Life is not fair!" As we judge the divorced woman who is remarrying, is part of our disapproval connected to being miserable in our own marriage but feeling stuck with it or to never having found that one soul mate we believe God promised us? Why should *she* have a second chance? Are we outraged at God for giving a healthy baby to a woman who once had an abortion while we sit childless and fill up an empty womb with the cancer of bitterness and regret?

Paul makes it very clear that those festering feelings and behaviors inhibit the growth of grace. "Get rid of all bitterness, rage and anger, brawling and slander, along with every form of malice. Be kind and compassionate to one another, forgiving each other, just as in Christ God forgave you" (Ephesians 4:31-32). Bitterness is a refusal to let go of something, some past wound or disappointment. Rage and anger can explode onto the canvas of another's life without warning or can be a menacing fire on slow burn, always at the back of our minds. Brawling and slander encompass a spirit to fight or damage the life of someone else with our words. Malice is perhaps the most damaging to our own souls. It is a desire to see someone suffer. You hear that marriage number two has ended, and you are glad. The woman who is expecting a child miscarries, and although you would never voice it to yourself or anyone else, you silently rejoice.

Grace calls us to think and live very differently. When the poison of un-grace flows in a family, it is deeply destructive to a marriage and to children. We pass on that kind of hate whether we mean to or not.

One of the challenges in my life is extending grace to my husband. I find it easy to extend grace to our son. I find it easy to extend grace to friends. I count it a privilege to extend grace to the women who stand in line for hours at my book table, waiting to tell someone their secrets. But I often struggle to show that same kindness to Barry. I justify my miserly spirit in my own mind by saying that I'm tired or that he never listens or that if he cared about my feelings, he wouldn't keep doing the same things over and over.

Then one day I heard myself in Christian. "Dad, you never listen!" The small voice was his, but the tone, the words were mine. I realized in split-second horror that I was passing on my lack of grace to our son.

Grace is not possible without the power of the indwelling Spirit of God. It is simply not in us. Watch the news on television, flick through talk shows or the current fad of 'sue your family on national television' dramas, and it is clear that we live in a world of un-grace. It is easy to fall to the level of the lowest common denominator, but Paul urges us to resist that in our homes and in our churches. "Then we will no longer be infants, tossed back and forth by the waves, and blown here and there by every wind of teaching and by the cunning and craftiness of men in their deceitful scheming. Instead, speaking the truth in love, we will in all things grow up into him who is the Head, that is, Christ" (Ephesians 4:14-15).

"We will in all things grow up." That's hard. When we are surrounded with pettiness and personal slights, we want to respond in kind. But what kind of house do you really want to build?

BUILDING UP OR TEARING DOWN?

In the spring of 2000, Barry and I and my father-in-law, William, bought a house together. William had been living with us since his wife, Eleanor, had died. He had kept his house in Charleston, South Carolina, for some time but decided to sell it. We decided to sell ours and together buy a bigger house. We looked for several months to find just the right place. We needed a house with enough bedrooms for us and a guest bedroom and room for an office for Barry and our assistant, Pat Sands. Finally we found the one. It seemed perfect, and we moved in.

One night there was a terrible storm. I was in my bedroom packing for a trip when Christian came running in very excited. "Look, Mom, it's raining!" He was soaked to the skin.

"Christian, you are not to go outside on a night like this!" I reprimanded him.

"I wasn't outside!" he shouted with glee as he raced back to the den. I followed him. Water was pouring in everywhere. Great puddles collected on the hardwood floors. We all pitched in with buckets and towels, but it was a disaster.

The next morning we called the builder. He came over with some men to look at the roof and the windows. "Wow, I've never built a house before that leaked as much as this one," he said. He sounded proud. They worked on it for a couple of days until the next storm. The leaks were worse. William called me upstairs to look at his bathroom ceiling. Water was pouring through a large crack in the corner. Water was dripping from another crack above his bathtub.

The list of disasters became almost comical. The first time the lawn sprinkler system came on, I was at the front door getting a package. The water jets shot over my head and into the hall, soaking the hardwood floor. I called the builder. "Yep! That's too far," he said. He was the master of understatement.

His crew repaired a window that was leaking in Christian's playroom. It was obviously a child's room, as toys were everywhere. I checked the window after the repairmen left and found thirty-seven nails on the floor. I called the builder. "Do you see what I have to put up with!" he said. He was not an edifying builder.

"Do not let any unwholesome talk come out of your mouths, but only what is helpful for building others up according to their needs, that it may benefit those who listen" (Ephesians 4:29). The "building others up" phrase Paul uses here comes from the Greek word for house builder. Paul's implication is that we have a choice in our heads, in our families, everywhere we go, to be a house builder or a house destroyer. The words we use and the body language we display will either build up or tear down. We get to choose, but we can't do it on our own.

Christian used my words and tone to talk to his dad, thinking, I assume, *If Mom does this, it must be okay.* How could I discipline behavior that was in essence my son's modeling me? As a flawed sinner I can't change, but as a daughter of the King, a woman whose sin was covered on Calvary and who is promised the power of the indwelling Holy Spirit of God, I can. Real change requires a daily yielding of myself to him, as I let my life be transformed by his presence within me.

That understanding was a huge breakthrough for me. I spent the first twenty-five years of my Christian life trying to do things *for* God. I was a miserable failure. Then I began to understand that I had missed the whole point. I don't do things *for* God; I do things *in* him. In *his* power, not my own. If we had been able to redeem ourselves, there would have been no need for the slaughter on Golgotha. The reality is that we can't change ourselves. There is nothing good in us, only Christ.

"In the same way, count yourselves dead to sin but alive to God in Christ Jesus" (Romans 6:11). Grace can completely transform the landscape of our lives and our families. Grace requires us to let go of petty grievances, the "that's not fair" refrain, the demand for our own rights, our compulsion to be right. Grace attacks us at the most primal level: our pride. We hate to think that there is nothing we can add to what God has done.

I see this raw human pride in Christian. Children who have not been shamed don't even try to hide their massive, intact ego. Christian still believes he is the best at everything he tries, that when he gets up in the morning the sun begins to shine, that the fact he's a winner inherently means everyone else loses.

We were in the park one day, playing in a sandbox. A boy about Christian's age came over and asked if he could borrow the rake Christian was using, which, incidentally, was park property. Christian said no. I asked him to share. He said no. I told him if he didn't share, we were going home. We went home. We talked about the incident later.

"Christian, the whole world does not revolve around you," I said.

"But I want it to," he replied with the candid honesty of a child.

Grace and pride are diametrically opposed. They cannot both enter the Kingdom of heaven. It is our privilege and calling to live with our arms outstretched, ready to build up those around us with love rather than tear them down with shame.

I had a very humbling encounter with a friend recently where the condition of my heart was exposed and grace was extended to me in my unloveliness. In 2000 I wrote a book called *Living Fearlessly*. In it I referred to several friends who had lived through experiences with the death of a child that were unthinkable to me. I wrote about the impact their lives were having on mine.

I had finished the book and printed off the relevant passages to send to each friend to make sure I had quoted them accurately. I was on a very tight deadline and was eager to get a green light to proceed. One of my friends faxed her copy back to me with so many changes it reminded me of papers my English teacher returned to me. I received it late at night, and I was tired and fed up with the whole process of writing. I could understand some of the changes she wanted, as they were important details about the loss of her beautiful child, but others seemed trivial to me in my weary arrogance.

I sent the pages back to her, telling her I would make the big changes but asking if she could live with the smaller details remaining the same. She said no; each detail was important to her. Rather than sit up all night making the changes, I decided I would just take her story out. I told my friend so, then e-mailed my editor and asked him to remove the two or three relevant paragraphs so I could meet my deadline. I knew I was wrong, which just made me more determined to stick to my guns.

As that week went on, I felt sick about the incident, but I was too stubborn and childish to try to put things straight. Finally I called my friend and asked her if we could meet for coffee. My agenda was simple: I would explain to her what my schedule was like and why I had done what I had done. I wanted to leave the meeting feeling better about myself. Driving to meet her, I knew my heart wasn't right, but I was stuck, so I prayed. I asked God to give me his ears to hear and his eyes to see.

When I arrived at the coffee shop, she was already there, and she got up and hugged me. My hug was a little more distant than usual because I was clutching my self-righteous baggage to my chest. I began to talk. I gave a very convincing, well-crafted speech. Then my friend spoke. As she talked about the agony of the loss of her darling child, the scales fell from my eyes and ears, and I was overwhelmed at my sinful behavior. She explained why every detail was etched in her mind with a pen of pain as her family savored every moment of life they had left with their daughter.

Tears poured down my cheeks as I saw myself clearly: my insensitivity, my lack of grace. All I could say was, "I am so sorry. I deeply regret wounding you. Can you ever forgive me?"

The fragrance of Christ flowed across the table as she reached out to me and forgave me wholeheartedly. I left that coffee shop overwhelmed at the grace of God and my friend and sobered by my sin and the damaging ripples of un-grace. When I got home, I called my editor and explained what had happened and asked if we could put the passages with all my friend's changes back in the book. I was making his life very difficult too. Again I encountered grace as he immediately agreed to make the changes.

LIVING IN THE LIGHT

That night I was sitting outside watching the sunset. Christian came and sat beside me. "Hi, Mom!" he said snuggling up close.

"Hi, darling," I replied. "How was your day?"

"Good," he said. "I caught four bugs and a butterfly in my net."

"Wow! That's a great day," I agreed.

"How was your day, Mom?" he asked.

"Bad and good," I answered.

"What part was bad?" he asked.

I told him that I had hurt a friend of mine and then didn't want to put it right. He asked me what part was good.

"Well, God changed my heart, and my friend forgave me," I said.

"Did she give you a time-out?" he wanted to know.

"No, she let me back in," I said.

That's what grace does. It unlocks the door out of the dark places we find ourselves in and lets us back into the light of God's presence. It does for us what we cannot do for ourselves. Left to myself I would have stayed the same. My friend would have remained wounded by my words and actions, and her story would not have been able to reach through the pages of that one book and be a beacon of hope to others who experience loss. But thanks be to God, we are not left alone. Just as God looked down on Jacob asleep in his deception and smiled down on him, just as Christ opened the door to a future for a woman tossed as refuse before him, God lovingly removed the blinders from this "woman of faith" and extended grace to me with outstretched arms.

He longs to do the same for you. Where the world and the church might close the door on us, Christ pays the ransom and throws the door open wide. That is a wonderful legacy to pass on to our children. Even as we allow them to feel the weight of sin and bad choices, we can share the grace of a love so big that every day is a brand-new page and the scrawls of yesterday are gone.

It's like the story of the pastor who met a young boy carrying a birdcage with three frightened birds shivering at the bottom. He asked the boy what he intended to do with them.

"Torment them a bit," he said. "I'll pull out some of their feathers and then give them to the cat."

"How much do you want for them?" the pastor asked.

"What do you want with them?" he asked. "They're not very pretty, and they don't even sing."

"How much?"

"Ten dollars."

The pastor gave the boy the ransom, set the cage on the ground, and released the birds.

He continued with his story, comparing it to the redemptive work of Christ. He imagined that one day Satan came into the presence of Christ. He had just returned from the Garden of Eden with a prize: the human race.

"How much do you want for them?" Jesus asked.

"All your tears and all your blood," Satan replied.

"Done."

In reality Satan did not have the power to demand a ransom from Christ. The price had to be paid to God himself. Christ paid it to set us free.

That is the gospel of grace. The ransom has been delivered, the price paid, the door opened. Religion gives us baggage; Jesus gives us wings.

Sitting all alone now, broken dreams
And in this place, this pretty cage, broken wings.
You're so afraid to fall again
But all you need is found in him
For you were made to rise upon the wind.

It's time for you to fly.
It's time to soar on eagle wings.
Don't be afraid, you're not alone so lift your head up high.
It's time for you to fly.

Take a look outside now and see the sky.
Can you hear all heaven sing, come and fly!
So take a step outside the door.
He paid the price, there's so much more
For you were made to rise upon the wind.

It's time for you to fly.
It's time to soar on eagle wings.
Don't be afraid, you're not alone so lift your head up high.
It's time for you to fly. (Sheila Walsh, John Hartley, Gary Saddler)

Grace is a risky business. If we understand it, if we embrace it, we will never be the same. I have heard it defined like this: Grace declares us worthy before we become worthy. That is what happened to me within the walls of a psychiatric hospital. I understood for the first time in my life that I had nothing to offer God but my broken, sinful self—and that was all he had ever wanted. I still struggle to let that whole glorious truth sink in.

"Do you mean there is nothing I can do to make God love me more?"

"Do you mean that any good thing in me did not come from me but is really God in me?"

"Do you mean that the shame I feel inside, the sense that I will never be enough, can be traded for a shame-free, worthy life in Christ?"

For the child who lies, there is a price to pay…but grace and love open a door to sunlight rather than shaming that child into the shadows. For the boy with dirty magazines under his bed, there is honest, open talk about the consequences of certain choices and the call to a pure heart…but grace and love open a door to sunlight rather than shaming that boy into the shadows. For the college girl who discovers that her childhood is over and she now carries a child, there are tough decisions to be made; life will never be the same…but grace and love open a door to sunlight rather shaming that young woman into the shadows.

In *Shame and Grace,* Lewis Smedes describes what a world like that might look like. I like to think of it as a statement of faith for our children.

> I believe that the only self I need to live up to is the self my
>   Maker meant me to be.
> I believe that I am accepted by the grace of God without regard
>   to my deserving.
> I believe that the grace of God heals the shame I do deserve and
>   heals the shame I don't.
> I believe that grace is the best thing in the world!

Forgiveness

When I survey the wondrous cross
On which the Prince of glory died,
My richest gain I count but loss,
And pour contempt on all my pride.

Were the whole realm of nature mine,
That were a present far too small;
Love so amazing, so divine,
Demands my soul, my life, my all.

—Isaac Watts, "When I Survey
   the Wondrous Cross"

3

═ FORGIVENESS ═

LOVE ON ITS KNEES

Bear with each other and forgive whatever grievances
you may have against one another. Forgive as the Lord forgave you.
And over all these virtues put on love,
which binds them all together in perfect unity.

COLOSSIANS 3:13-14

It is hard to make your adversaries real people unless you recognize
yourself in them—in which case, if you don't watch out,
they cease to be adversaries.

FLANNERY O'CONNOR

"How many is seventy times seven, Mom?" Christian asked one day as we sat on the deck waiting for the arrival of the evening's fireflies.

"Four hundred and ninety," I replied. "Why do you ask?"

"Miss Dawn says that we have to forgive seventy times seven."

"That's right," I said, thanking God once more in my heart for Christian's preschool teacher.

"That's a lot," he said.

"It is a lot," I agreed. "But just think of all the things that Jesus forgives in us."

"So after four hundred and ninety I don't have to forgive anymore?" he asked.

"Well, that's not the point really," I said. "Jesus asks us to keep on forgiving."

"Then why did he say seventy times seven?"

"Well...to show how far forgiveness should go," I said.

"I still think that's too much. I think that's too much for Trevor," he said, naming a classmate whose name has been changed to protect the feelings of Trevor's mom!

That's exactly how Peter felt. "Then Peter came to Jesus and asked, 'Lord, how many times shall I forgive my brother when he sins against me? Up to seven times?' Jesus answered, 'I tell you, not seven times, but seventy-seven times'" (Matthew 18:21-22). The issue at stake here is personal forgiveness. The consensus in rabbinic tradition was that a person might be forgiven a repeated sin three times; on the fourth, there was no forgiveness. So Peter volunteered to go way overboard and forgive seven times. I imagine he thought that Jesus would give him a big thumbs-up for his largeness of heart in going to such extremes. That's not the response he received. Instead Jesus taught a parable illustrating that we have all been forgiven far more than we will ever be asked to forgive.

EXTREME PARDON

In Matthew 18 Jesus told the story of a king who was getting his financial house in order, calling in all outstanding debts. One of his servants owed him ten thousand talents, a huge amount of money. The servant couldn't pay his debt, so the king ordered that the servant and his wife and children be sold until he could pay back what he owed. This was a common and acceptable Old Testament practice. But the top price for a slave was only one talent. Clearly there was no way this man could save himself or his family. He begged for more time to repay his debt, but what would time buy him? How could a servant ever raise that kind of money?

Then a miracle happened. The king had pity on his servant and forgave the huge debt. Can you imagine what that would have been like? If you have ever faced severe financial pressure, you know it can be overwhelming. After I left the Christian Broadcasting Network, I was paid disability for one year as I battled clinical depression. I assumed that taxes were taken out of my monthly check just as they had been when I received a regular salary. I was wrong. When my taxes were prepared the following April, I discovered that I owed the government a lot of money I didn't have.

I drove away from the tax office in shock. I pulled over to the side of the road and wept. I couldn't see any way out. I couldn't believe I had been so foolish. Thank God for the ways he rescues us! A good friend stepped in and paid the bill for me and gave me as much time as I needed to pay her back. Take my situation, and multiply it over and over, and we see the plight of the king's indebted servant. No friend in his world would have been able to help him out if the king had not forgiven him. I can envision him running home, light as air, free as a balloon released from the hand of a carefree child, grabbing his wife and spinning her round and round the kitchen, laughing the belly laugh of the suddenly ransomed.

But that is not how the story goes. The king's kindness changed the servant's situation but not his heart. "But when that servant went out, he found one of his fellow servants who owed him a hundred denarii. He grabbed him and began to choke him. 'Pay back what you owe me!' he demanded" (Matthew 18:28).

His fellow servant owed him a minuscule amount compared to what he had owed the king. But when his peer couldn't pay the debt, the ungrateful servant had him thrown in debtor's prison. This was illegal, for even the cheapest slaves sold for five hundred denarii, and it was against the law to sell a man for more than he owed.

When the king heard what had transpired, he called the forgiven servant "wicked." He bypassed the mere imprisonment option and ordered that the man be tortured until he could pay his debt in full—which would be never!

The message is clear: We have been forgiven more than we could ever forgive. Whatever anyone does to us pales in comparison to what our sin has already done to Christ. The servant could do nothing to earn the king's compassion. It was a gift. When he refused to extend that same gift to another, the forgiveness he had been granted was revoked. Those who are forgiven must forgive, or they stand incapable of receiving forgiveness. Jesus ended his account of the king and his servant with these chilling words: "This is how my heavenly Father will treat each of you unless you forgive your brother from your heart" (Matthew 18:35).

"WHOSE SIDE ARE YOU ON?"

Perhaps my son would find it easier to forgive his friend if Trevor were really sorry, but it galls Christian to be expected to forgive someone who isn't sorry at all. I find that galling too. But how sorry are we? I am convinced that most of us have no concept of what we have been delivered from or what our sin cost Christ. And it is impossible to appreciate how much we are loved unless we realize how much we have been forgiven.

Christ said of Mary Magdalene, "Therefore, I tell you, her many sins have been forgiven—for she loved much. But he who has been forgiven little loves little" (Luke 7:47). I think what Jesus was saying is that Mary understood how great her need was for forgiveness and so her love for Christ was great. Most of us don't understand how great our need is or how much we have been forgiven, and that is reflected in our small love.

Asking forgiveness in prayer can easily become rote, a simple wiping the slate clean. My daily challenge as a parent is to model and teach my son principles and concepts that have no earthly precedent or earthly hope without Christ. I tell him to forgive a boy who pushed him into a puddle, and he looks at me as if to say, "What's wrong with you,

Mom? You're supposed to be on my side!" It's at this point I grasp the truth that we forgive because Christ has told us to, and if we refuse, unforgiveness eats at our souls like the corrosive drip, drip, drip of battery acid. We lock ourselves behind the bars of our own resentment.

Two survivors of a Nazi prisoner-of-war camp sat having a conversation years after their liberation. "Have you forgiven the Nazis?" one friend asked the other.

"Yes."

"Well, I have not. I am still consumed with hatred for them."

"In that case," his friend said gently, "they still have you in prison."

A friend of mine is a very committed member of Alcoholics Anonymous. AA's "Big Book" identifies the "'number one' offender" for the alcoholic as resentment. I was astonished to hear that. I would have thought that alcohol wielded a heavier sword. But the founders of AA contend that from resentments "stem all forms of spiritual disease." The "Big Book" goes on to say, "It is plain that a life which includes deep resentment leads only to futility and unhappiness. To the precise extent that we permit these, do we squander the hours that might have been worthwhile.... For when harboring such feelings we shut ourselves off from the sunlight of the Spirit."

Resentment is a "looking back," a clinging to the past, a refusal to let go. In resentment we revisit the hurt, the feelings of powerlessness, the rage, and nurse it like a sick infant until we live more in the past than in the present. Simmering resentment hinders healthy anger as it refuses to let go and move on. It numbs us to the underlying feelings of pain and sadness that we have to be willing to face in order to heal. Resentment is a roadblock that only God can remove.

I think of a phone conversation I had with a woman who was stuck in a sea of pain and anger over her husband's infidelity. She nursed it. She picked at it like a child eager to see what lies beneath a scab. She picked at it partly out of fear that it would heal and leave her looking whole when inside she was in tatters.

Her husband had told her recently that unless she could start to forgive him and let them begin a new life together, then he would leave her.
She called me because she was so torn inside and eaten up by resentment and rage. As we talked, I learned that her father had abandoned
her as a child, and now the actions of her husband had tapped into all
the unresolved pain and loss she'd carried for years. I asked her how long
ago her husband's infidelity had occurred and whether it was an incident or a long-term relationship.

"It was four years ago," she said. "It was a one-night stand."

"Do you want to forgive him?" I asked.

"No!" she said vehemently.

"Why?" I pressed gently.

"Because that will make it okay, and it's not okay. It will never be
okay!" she cried.

I assured her that extending forgiveness doesn't make sin okay.
Rather, releasing anger and resentment lets *us* out of prison. Forgiveness
is the antidote to the poison of bitterness. Forgiving is a process. We
take the smallest step. We take one more. It is a commitment to walk on
a certain path. It is, as Eugene Peterson says, "a long obedience in the
same direction."

"WHAT WOULD YOU HAVE DONE?"

The title of Simon Wiesenthal's book *The Sunflower* does not prepare
you for the content. I picked it up imagining myself welcomed into a
warm and tender story and was confronted instead with a brutal tale.
The book chronicles the experience of a Jewish prisoner at the hands of
his Nazi captors during World War II. Every time I read the story, I am
reminded that even when we feel no obligation to forgive, if we don't,
we are haunted by our own bitter resentment and our inability to let go
of the past.

Simon Wiesenthal lost more than eighty members of his extended family through the most inhumane torture imaginable, but he survived the prison camps and years later wrote this book. *The Sunflower* is written as a question: "Should I have forgiven him? What would you have done?" The "him" in question was a young Nazi soldier who, on his deathbed, turned to Simon as a confessor. Simon was on latrine duty when a nurse fetched him and ordered him to stand by the bedside of a dying soldier of the Third Reich. Through bandages that made his face unrecognizable, the soldier told Simon everything he had done or been a part of in brutalizing the Jewish people in the camps. He then asked Simon to forgive him and explained that he couldn't die in peace unless he'd been able to ask a Jew for forgiveness. Simon was disgusted by what he heard and revolted by the idea that a deathbed confession could wipe clean such a bloody slate. He pulled his arm from the grip of the wounded man and left the room. A few hours later the soldier died.

After the war Simon was drawn to the home of that soldier. What were his parents like? Had the soldier told the truth when he said he was raised by parents who loved and honored God? The dead soldier's mother answered the door and informed Simon that both her son and husband were dead. "Did you know my son?" she asked. "He was a good boy."

Simon couldn't bring himself to tell the mother the atrocities that her son had been part of. He left her in peace with her memories intact. But he was left with his question: "Should I have forgiven him? If you had been in my place, what would you have done?"

I have wondered if Simon's refusal to forgive actually contributed to saving that young man's eternal soul. In those remaining hours with a soul burdened with guilt, did the Nazi go to the only One who has the power to forgive sin? Surely the soldier was asking the wrong person in the first place.

The Sunflower highlights the difference in the understanding of forgiveness between Jew and Christian. Denis Prager, a talk-show host in Los Angeles, is a religious Jew and the author of many books. He says that for the Jew forgiveness can come only from the person who has been wronged. Therefore, there is no forgiveness for murder, as the person who was killed is gone. God will only forgive if the person wronged has forgiven first. Prager observes a nation where murder is rife and asks whether the Christian view of forgiveness, where all can be forgiven, has damaged our country. Americans seem to take sin so lightly.

I find that an intriguing thought. Perhaps the dilemma is that for a Jew who has committed what to him is the unforgivable sin, there is nowhere to go, while for the Christian the very things that nailed Christ to the cross are taken too lightly. How seriously do we take Paul's words, "You are not your own; you were bought at a price" (1 Corinthians 6:19-20)?

Only divine love and grace make forgiveness possible. The love of God compels us to forgive. The grace of God makes us willing to. Left to myself I echo Christian's sentiments, "What's wrong with you, God? You're supposed to be on my side!"

We are called to love, but how can we love without the grace of God? We are called to extend grace, but how can we do that without the love of God? We are called to forgive those who have harmed us, but how can we do that without the love and grace of God? When love, grace, and forgiveness hold hands, I am sure heaven applauds and the Father says, "They are beginning to understand."

"WHAT ARE YOU DOING, LORD?"

"How long, O LORD, must I call for help, but you do not listen? Or cry out to you, 'Violence!' but you do not save? Why do you make me look at injustice? Why do you tolerate wrong?" (Habakkuk 1:2-3).

The popularity of his name may have died out, but Habakkuk's question lives on: "What are you doing, Lord? Don't you see what is happening all around me?" When I look back on my own history, I am grateful for the faithfulness of God in so many diverse situations. I see how he has delivered me from hopelessness and fear. But I have bruised my knees on the altar of my unforgiveness. I have to come back again and again.

Clinical depression is still misunderstood and unacceptable in certain circles within the church. I found that out when I was weak and broken and the response of some people I had counted as friends almost overwhelmed me. I had three, like Job's comforters, who condemned me in different ways. One wrote me a letter while I was still a patient in the psychiatric unit, suggesting that I was using this "phony" illness as an excuse to take a break from my life. He urged me to stop pretending to be sick. Another "friend" said that I was a compulsive liar and wouldn't know what was true if it hit me in the face. He said I should never be allowed back into any form of public ministry. The third friend has not spoken to me from that day until this, over ten years later.

When I was at the bottom mentally and emotionally, I had never felt more lonely in my life. I have never felt more unworthy of love before or since. My friends' words to me were like earth on top of a casket in my soul. "If an enemy were insulting me, I could endure it; if a foe were raising himself against me, I could hide from him. But it is you, a man like myself, my companion, my close friend, with whom I once enjoyed sweet fellowship" (Psalm 55:12-14). I didn't know what to do.

Then I was confronted with Jesus' command to forgive. Over time I attempted to contact all three of the people who had hurt me so deeply. My first friend and I were able to talk things through and come to a place of understanding, deeper friendship, and mutual forgiveness. The second person maintained his position that I was much sicker than I knew and would never be restored. I have tried to contact the third person, but she will not respond.

I have come to understand that forgiveness is something I choose to do out of obedience to God whether I want to or not, whether I feel like it or not. That's how I began to leave my interior prison. In prayer I began forgiving the people who'd hurt me, even though I didn't mean a word of it. I was clear with God about that. "Lord, you know me well. I want to forgive because you ask me to, but I am so angry and hurt. I choose now to drag my will in line with yours and forgive. Help me. Give me your heart and your eyes. Amen."

That's how I started. It was pretty pathetic, but it was all I had. If I had waited until I wanted to forgive, I would still be waiting. I've found liberty in obedience. I have also experienced humility. For me it's saying to God, "I don't understand your ways, but I say yes! to them. You are right, I am wrong. I don't always see how, but I believe it to be true." This is a "drop-your-rock moment," as Nicole Johnson says. That's hard for me to grasp as a forty-four-year-old. It's even more difficult to communicate to a four-year-old.

"IT'S TOO HEAVY"

"Do you want to forgive Trevor?" I asked Christian as we sat under the stars with a jar full of fireflies.

"No, Mom. I don't want to forgive him," he replied honestly.

"I understand that," I said. "Come into the kitchen for a moment. I want to give you something." He followed me in, wondering what kind of treat might be in store.

"Hold this," I said as I placed a two-pound bag of flour in his hands.

"What are we going to do, Mom?" he asked.

"I want you to carry it around."

"Why?"

"Just carry it for a while." I told him. "Let's go back outside, but bring your bag of flour."

"Can I put it down now?" he asked when we decided a bit later to go for a walk.

"No, not yet," I said.

"But it's heavy!"

"I know. Come on."

After ten minutes he'd had it. "I'm putting it down now, Mom!" he said. "It's too heavy."

I took it from him. My parable was simple: When we won't forgive, we carry the weight of our resentment around with us.

"When you won't forgive Trevor," I explained to my son, "it's like carrying a bag inside your heart with Trevor's name on it. Jesus will help you put it down even if Trevor won't."

Put your unforgiveness down; it's too heavy.

In their best-selling book *Boundaries,* Drs. Henry Cloud and John Townsend write, "Nothing clarifies boundaries more than forgiveness. When you refuse to forgive someone, you still want something from that person, and even if it is revenge that you want, it keeps you tied to him forever." When we forgive, we let it go; we cut the tie that holds us to the one who has wounded us. It's like the powerful visual illustration in the movie *The Mission.* Robert De Niro's character drags his heavy bags up the mountainside, falling again and again, refusing help from anyone as he attempts to atone for his sin. Finally he reaches the top, one of the natives cuts him free, and the bags fall back down the mountain. He and his rescuer laugh and laugh till tears of joyful relief pour down De Niro's face.

Forgiveness does that. It cuts the ties and lets the burden roll back down the mountain.

Old Testament theology seems to give more space to our human sense of justice. The old eye for an eye, tooth for a tooth chess game appears to have provided rules that were clear to everyone, but grace cleared the board, and the only rule that remains is love. "The entire law is summed up in a single command: 'Love your neighbor as yourself'" (Galatians 5:14). And love demands forgiveness.

Just as babies learn to love by being loved, children learn to forgive by being forgiven. Dr. Paul Faulkner surveyed thirty families for his book *Raising Faithful Kids in a Fast-Paced World*. The goal: to look at what was working and what wasn't working for Christian families as they parented their children late in the twentieth century. He tells the story of a family whose son messed up so badly that he ended up in prison. The boy had been in trouble before, and this was the last straw for his father. As his son's release date approached, the dad spent some time with his pastor, discussing how to help the boy straighten up.

"I'm really going to tighten up on discipline this time," the father asserted.

The pastor reminded him of the return of another troubled boy who was greeted not with a tighter ship but with a party. Amazingly, the father agreed to try this approach. When the boy arrived home, he saw cars in the driveway, balloons and streamers everywhere, and a "Welcome home!" banner.

Dr. Faulkner asked the pastor how things worked out for the family. "Well, I haven't talked to the family much recently, but I see them in church every Sunday. That boy sits with his folks, with his arm around his mom."

Forgiveness with grace. This dad's forgiveness opened the door to another way of life for his son and his family. Forgiveness says, "I believe you can live differently and make better choices; I still believe in you." I don't think there is anything more soul destroying for a child than the loss of hope. Forgiveness tucks hope in a child's back pocket like a gift from a sweet aunt on Christmas Day. Some might be skeptical of this kind of approach, but love, grace, and forgiveness seem to have won the day in this family.

"I'M SO SORRY"

Forgiving someone can be terribly difficult. Asking someone for forgiveness can be even harder. It is a powerful thing, however, when a parent asks a child for forgiveness, no matter what the age of the "child."

I will never forget such a moment with my mother. She flew over from Scotland to Washington, D.C. while I was in the psychiatric hospital there. She stayed in a local hotel and joined me a couple of times in therapy sessions. My counselor began to talk to Mom about the time leading up to my father's stay in a psychiatric unit and his subsequent death at thirty-five. I listened to her talk about the pain, the fear, the uncertainty of the time. Then she began to cry, and I realized for the first time that she had carried guilt for years. She wondered if she had allowed my dad to stay in the house too long, if it had caused damage to me that she could have prevented. She turned to me and said with deep feeling, "I'm so sorry."

I will never forget that moment. I don't believe that my mom could have done anything different. I know she did her best with the knowledge and help she had at the time. But it meant the world to me to hear her say she was sorry. And I assured her I forgave her. The act of asking for forgiveness and the act of forgiving placed us side by side at the foot of the cross. We found each other in humility.

Barry and I practice making amends to Christian. He is just a little boy, but he knows when we are wrong or inconsistent. It is a joy to humble oneself before a child and to become childlike as a result. "And he said: 'I tell you the truth, unless you change and become like little children, you will never enter the kingdom of heaven. Therefore, whoever humbles himself like this child is the greatest in the kingdom of heaven'" (Matthew 18:3-4).

I laughed at something Christian did recently. I thought he meant it to be funny, but he didn't, and I hurt his feelings. He disappeared into the dining room, and I found him under the table.

"Can I come in?" I asked.

"No, I want to be alone."

I tried again a little later. "Can I come in now?"

"Okay," he said.

"Christian, I hurt your feelings, and I am so sorry. Will you please forgive me?"

"I forgive you, Mommy," he said crawling over beside me.

If I took his feelings lightly, would he confide in me the next time I wounded him? And I certainly will wound him. I'm his mommy and would die for him, but I'm human, and I will hurt him no matter how hard I try not to.

Asking forgiveness is not about us; it's about the one we have wounded. I don't need to understand or agree that what I said was wrong. If I have hurt another, that's enough for me to know. If I, with Paul, want to be a house builder, then the mortar of repentance and forgiveness is essential.

While forgiveness is our calling, the wings to our freedom, we need to keep in mind that we cannot control the outcome of the forgiveness process. I spent some time with a woman who was bitterly disillusioned with God. "My husband left me for another woman," she confided. "He left our three kids. I was devastated. I prayed and prayed. Then one day he called and asked if he could come to the house and talk to me. I just knew that God had answered my prayers."

She paused for a moment as though the memory was as fresh as if it had happened that day. "He asked me to forgive him. I said I would. I was over the moon. My family was back together! So I thought. He married that woman. He just wanted a clean slate for his new little life!"

It was obvious that this hurting woman felt betrayed by her husband and betrayed by God. "What was the point of my forgiving him if he left me anyway?" she said. "What message does that give to the kids?"

We talked for a long time. "You are in pain because of the choice he made," I said, "and more pain because you can't make him choose what you want him to choose. I can't imagine how agonizing that is. But you do get to choose for yourself how you'll live from this point on. Your children are watching you. You can model for them that you are a victim of the whims of a weak man, or you can show them that even in the darkest valley, even when others make bad choices, pain and resentment do not consume you. Even there God's love is *so* big."

Life is not fair, but through the gully of heartbreaking injustice flows God's river of mercy. The call to live out forgiveness before our children is as impossible as the call to live out love, to live out grace. It's impossible without the power of the indwelling Holy Spirit and a focus on Christ.

It is humbling to ask for forgiveness but not impossible when seen through the frame of the sacrifice of Christ. As he allowed his body to be nailed to the cross, he chose the ultimate humiliation and agony of separation from his Father. He offered his body as the punching bag for the sin of the world. He took every blow because he loves us. He drank the cup of the wrath of God, every last drop, so that we can be liberated, so that we can forgive and be forgiven. Such knowledge brings us to our knees.

Our Father in heaven,
hallowed be your name,
your kingdom come,
your will be done
    on earth as it is in heaven.
Give us today our daily bread.
Forgive us our debts,
    as we also have forgiven our debtors.
And lead us not into temptation,
but deliver us from the evil one. (Matthew 6:9-13)

Truth

Jesus bids us shine
With a clear, pure light,
Like a little candle
Burning in the night.
In this world of darkness,
So we must shine,
You in your small corner,
And I in mine.

—Susan Warner, "Jesus Bids Us Shine"

4

═ TRUTH ═

LOVE WITH INTEGRITY

Test me, O LORD, and try me, examine my heart and my mind;
for your love is ever before me, and I walk continually in your truth.

PSALM 26:2-3

Wherever there is truth, it is the Lord's.
JUSTIN MARTYR

"Our scholars say that at the Creation of man four angels stood as Godparents. The angels of Mercy, Truth, Peace and Justice. For a long time they disputed over whether God ought to create man at all. The strongest opponent was the angel of Truth. This angered God and as a punishment he sent him into banishment on the earth. But the other angels begged God to pardon him, and finally he listened and summoned the angel of Truth back to heaven. The angel brought back a clod of earth which was soaked in tears, tears that he had shed on being banished from heaven and from this clod of earth God created man."

No, this is not the Genesis account of Creation. It's a story shared by a Jewish man remembered only by his first name, Josek. One night during World War II, he and 149 other men lay huddled together in the stifling heat of a concentration camp in Germany. His friend Simon Wiesenthal, who relates this conversation in *The Sunflower,* says the issue up for discussion that night was "Are we all made from the same stuff?" Did God make the camp commandant out of the same material as a helpless child? Are we all capable of selfless good and unspeakable barbarity? Is the executed bomber of the federal building in Oklahoma City of the same value to God as an innocent child who lost her life when McVeigh's bomb of hatred and twisted sense of justice brought her nursery to its knees? Do we all start out the same, or are some of us predisposed to evil and some to good? Does God love us all equally?

When we look at the issues of truth and integrity, what we are capable of as human beings is an important question to address. Paul was intimately aware of his lack of truth and integrity apart from Christ. "I know that nothing good lives in me, that is, in my sinful nature. For I have the desire to do what is good, but I cannot carry it out. For what I do is not the good I want to do; no, the evil I do not want to do—this I keep on doing" (Romans 7:18-19). I take comfort in this moment of truth from Paul. We are all in the same boat. Apart from Christ we can do nothing good at all. This fact is offensive to some believers, but even Christ himself made it clear on numerous occasions that the good he did was from the Father, the words he spoke were from the Father. "So Jesus said, 'When you have lifted up the Son of Man, then you will know that I am the one I claim to be and that I do nothing on my own but speak just what the Father has taught me'" (John 8:28).

This is wonderful news if we can step over our pride to see it. Not even the Son of God could do anything on his own, but his life is a shining proclamation of what it looks like to surrender everything to the Father.

I didn't hear much about this growing up, did you? When I was five, we left the Scottish Brethren denomination and returned to my mother's Baptist roots. So I was brought up in a warm, loving, evangelical church, but the emphasis was on what we could do for God. I was either "climbing Jacob's ladder" or "in the Lord's army." Until the last few years I never understood that I couldn't do any of this by myself. I didn't understand that because of the love, grace, and forgiveness of God everything has *already been done,* and now I can put *trusting* in the place of *trying.* Think of the years of guilt and confusion we could spare our children if they understood that the life we are called to lead is a supernatural one and that we are not the superhero of our own story; Jesus is.

"I WANT TO DO THE RIGHT THING"

One night Barry, Christian, and I were at the mall. We decided to eat at the cafeteria before going home. I had no idea that cafeterias existed before we had a child, but the first time we took him out to eat in public, I realized my days of meandering through a quiet dinner were through. We went to a nice restaurant in Nashville with another couple who doesn't have children. Big mistake. By the time the third piece of pasta had been launched into orbit, I decided that Christian and I would play "count the birds in the parking lot."

I then embarked on a holy quest to find noisy places where we could blend in with the general maelstrom, and eureka! I discovered the cafeteria. On that particular evening at the mall, Christian was tired, and like all of us when we are tired, his resistance to his sinful nature was low. He dropped some blue Jell-O on the floor to see if it would bounce, kind of like a science project. Barry told him to pick it up.

"No, it's messy," he said.

"Take a spoon and pick it up, please. Do you expect James to pick up your messes?" Barry asked. (James is our friend who brings the ice-tea cart around, and every Tuesday night he dresses up as a different character. We have an exciting life!)

I knew we were at a high-noon moment. "No!" Christian said defiantly.

Father and son disappeared into the bathroom for a quiet moment together. When they reappeared, Christian's face was red, and big tears sat on the edge of his eyelashes, preparing to plunge down his velvet cheeks. We got into the car in silence and drove toward home. Halfway there, Christian started to cry out loud.

"I don't want to be like this," he said. "I want to do the right thing, but it's so hard. I don't want to be disobedient."

"I know, darling," I said. "Me neither."

That night we talked about how hard it is to do the right thing. "I struggle every day to do the right thing, Christian," I told him. "I can't do it on my own."

"But it's okay for you, Mom. No one's going to punish you," he said.

"That's not why we do the right thing, sweet pea," I continued. "We do it to please God."

"Will he punish you when you're disobedient?" he asked.

"It's not that God will punish me, Christian. Jesus has already paid for all of Mommy's sins and all of your sins. But I love God, and I *want* to do the right thing."

"So what do you do when you want to be naughty?"

"I ask God to help me," I said.

"What do you do if no one can see you?" he asked, hoping to have found a theological loophole.

"What we do when no one is looking is just as important as what we do when someone else can see," I told him.

He looked as if he wasn't quite convinced. I understood that. Integrity is a much maligned, undervalued virtue in our culture. It goes against our nature. What we can get away with seems to be the quest of the day. There is an irrevocable law of the universe, however, that we ignore at our own peril: We will reap what we sow. Consequences fall into different categories. For some serious crimes the consequences are imprisonment, lack of freedom. But what about those who escape detection? Are they really free?

Being found out doesn't seem to be the deciding factor when it comes to our souls. Guilt is a cancer of the soul, a robber of sleep, a gift to those large pharmaceutical companies that produce the numerous new medications for anxiety and depression. But one of our goals as parents is to raise godly children who will be able to leave us and continue to make good choices on their own. Barry and I want Christian to be able to stand on his own two feet and go into the future a good, moral man who in turn will be a loving husband and father.

How do we teach our children to tell the truth because it is right when those who lie and appear to benefit from it surround them? How do we teach them to value what is right and noble in a society that pays little homage to what is good and true? Consequences are where we begin. "If you do that again, you will have a time-out." "If you disobey, no television for a week."

In his book *The Parent Survival Guide,* clinical psychologist Dr. Todd Cartmell gives positive solutions to forty common problems parents face daily. On consequences, his advice is very practical. If I apply it to a conversation I had with my nephew when he was ten, it would go something like this…

"Okay, because of your rude, defiant behavior, there will be no Game Boy tonight and no television."

"That's not fair," he would reply.

At this point I have two choices. I can become embroiled in the "That's not fair" discussion, or I can say, "We'll talk about this later." Dr. Cartmell says that if we enter into that kind of discussion when emotions are high, it is a no-win situation; we are even rewarding bad behavior by the amount of attention we are giving the child at that point. He also says that the discussion should not take place immediately after the punishment is over. When we rush in to comfort after a time-out with a younger child or some other disciplinary action with an older child, that warm, forgiving moment is its own reward and may result in further acting out to get that kind of attention.

Cartmell also advocates helping children of any age to accept consequences by talking to them about consequences when there is no crisis. He suggests that every family should have a "Detour Method" that is age-appropriate for each child. That means that we provide our child with one or two sentences he can use internally when he is being disciplined. For an older child it might be "If I argue here, I'm going to end up in more trouble. We'll talk about it later." A younger child would need something simple: "I should listen to Mom. Okay." Christian and I have come up with a little formula that he likes. When he is being naughty and is sent to his room for a time-out, he says to himself, "Stop. Breathe. Think." It seems to work for him, and to be honest, I've tried it myself, and it works for me, too!

External consequences are important. "He who ignores discipline comes to poverty and shame, but whoever heeds correction is honored" (Proverbs 13:18). But administering wise discipline is not enough. Our privilege as parents is to live out the love of God before our children in such a compelling way that they will choose the narrow path with a heart bent on honoring God above all others.

Christian and I finished our bedtime conversation. "You can't do the right things on your own, Christian," I said. "You have to ask Jesus to help you. That's what Mommy and Daddy do. God loves us all the time. The way we show him that we love him too is to come to him every day for everything, and when we make a bad choice, we ask him to forgive us. It's like your Magna Doodle. He'll wipe your slate clean when you ask him to. (Magna Doodle is a child's magnetic writing board that can be wiped clean with a simple shake.)

"But *how* will he help me?" Christian asked.

"Well, he will live in your heart, twenty-four hours a day, seven days a week, and if you ask him to help you make good choices, he will," I said.

He thought about that for a few moments. "Now you tell me!" he said.

A LEAKY SHELTER

I struggled with telling the truth as a child. In retrospect I think my reason was that I felt as if my value as a person was based on being liked. If I had done something wrong, I would deny it rather than face up to what I'd done. In my mind a bad thing equaled a bad person, and no one likes a bad person. But I hated that about myself. The legacy of living like that is that you are convinced the only reason you have any friends is because no one knows the truth about you. The shelter I built to protect myself was by nature leaky.

Sometimes I lied to fit in.

"Have you heard the new Eagles album?"

"Yes, it's great," I would reply. (Just don't ask me anything about it, because I didn't even know they had a new project.)

That kind of behavior is based on sinful and flawed information. Do you catch yourself in lies and then have to cover with bigger ones?

We lie because we don't want to get caught.

We lie because we are ashamed of our behavior.

We lie because we feel inadequate.

We lie because we want to make ourselves seem more interesting than we perceive ourselves to be.

The liberating truth, however, is that we have all been "caught," and Christ has paid the consequences. He took our guilt and shame upon himself so we could drop our false fronts. We are inadequate, but in Christ we have all things. There is great peace and winsomeness about people who are comfortable in their own shoes because they know they are loved.

For me a large part of the challenge of developing character and integrity is accepting that my sufficiency is not in me, Barry, Christian, my home, my job, or anything else. My sufficiency is in God alone. Everything else is a poor substitute, an impostor, and a disappointment.

David recognized this. I see Psalm 63 as a psalm to sustain me in a world where truth is scarce and integrity and character are continually undermined. This is my daily prayer.

> O God, you are my God,
>   earnestly I seek you;
> my soul thirsts for you,
>   my body longs for you,
> in a dry and weary land
>   where there is no water.
> I have seen you in the sanctuary
>   and beheld your power and your glory.
> Because your love is better than life,
>   my lips will glorify you.
> I will praise you as long as I live,
>   and in your name I will lift up my hands.
> My soul will be satisfied as with the richest of foods;
>   with singing lips my mouth will praise you. (Psalm 63:1-5)

Surely we live in a dry and weary land. Our nation is tired. We change the guard in Washington, hoping that will bring the change we long for, but it never will, because the only change that sustains is the change that God can produce in a human heart. We are all desperately wicked—utterly human and imperfect—without him.

David says, "I have seen you in the sanctuary." I love this. David is one of the Old Testament saints who did not have a theophany, a physical encounter with God. Adam and Eve walked with God in the Garden of Eden, Jacob saw God at the top of the ladder, Moses had the burning bush. Many others in the Old Testament had a physical encounter with God, generally in human form. David did not. Perhaps, like me, you have reasoned at times that if only you could see God face to face, you would be different. Biblical history indicates that is not true.

What is true and gives all of us hope is that even without a face-to-face encounter, David could say, "I have *seen* you in the sanctuary." David's love for God sprang out of his *faith*. Because he believed everything he had been taught and had experienced about God, he declared with passion, "Your love is better than life." David, a sinful human being like the rest of us, knew where to place his trust—and it wasn't in a leaky shelter of his own making.

CHARACTER DEVELOPMENT

In their book *Raising Great Kids,* Drs. Henry Cloud and John Townsend define character as "the sum of our abilities to deal with life as God designed us to." We all have negative personality traits, however, that rear their ugly little heads from time to time.

One of mine is anger. I can cope with a lot, and then one day I've just had it, and watch out if you're in my way. Barry talked to me about this one day and said that it really bothered him and asked if I would discuss it with our counselor, Scot. That is one of our commitments to each other in our marriage. If we get stuck on an issue, we seek outside help from a godly therapist.

I told Scot that when I feel as if Barry isn't listening to me, occasionally I get mad and let him have it.

"Why do you do that?" Scot asked.

"Well, I feel as if he doesn't care about me," I said.

"Do you believe that you respond as God would have you respond?"

"Well…no. But sometimes I can't help it," I said pathetically.

"Yes, you can," he said.

"If I could, I wouldn't be here," I replied.

"That's not true, Sheila. The Holy Spirit of God lives in you to enable you to live differently. You can't change on your own, but you can change if you will bend your will to his will."

I left that day thinking, *That sounds easy until I'm in that place... but when I'm angry, I don't care about doing the right thing.* So that's where I started. "Lord Jesus," I prayed, "I have a problem. It's me. I get angry and wound with my words. Please help me to humble myself before you and choose to respond as you would respond."

The next time I found myself wanting to explode I locked myself in the bathroom. I don't remember reading that Christ ever locked himself in the bathroom, but it was all I could do. I got down on my knees and asked God to help me. It was not an overnight change, but God *is* changing me. As long as I see myself as a victim of my human nature, I will never change, but by God's grace I can drag my stubborn will in line with God's will, and he can transform me.

Cloud and Townsend divide character development into six stages: attachment, responsibility, reality, competence, conscience, and worship.

ATTACHMENT

"If we live, we live to the Lord; and if we die, we die to the Lord. So, whether we live or die, we belong to the Lord" (Romans 14:8).

I was baking cookies for Christian's class one day, and a television talk show was on in the background. The subject being discussed was belonging to gangs. One line stuck with me because it was a voluminous commentary on our society. When an eleven-year-old boy was asked why he ran with such a violent gang, he replied, "You have to belong somewhere."

I have heard that same sentiment expressed in diverse circles:

"The reason I joined Alcoholics Anonymous wasn't just to beat drinking. I wanted to be with others who would understand. I wanted to belong."

"I joined a cancer survivors group. I figured they would be the only ones who really know what it feels like to have your body invaded by an enemy."

"I'm in a men's accountability group to remind me that what I do matters. I'm not a lone ranger."

"I come to Women of Faith conferences because I love watching how the six speakers love each other. I want that. I want to feel that needed and important."

Healthy human attachment gives life context, meaning, and dignity. Without it our souls shrivel up. Christian's tears on our car trip home from the mall were because he loves us and knew he had made the wrong choice. What matters to us matters to him because we are bonded in relationship.

RESPONSIBILITY

"I said, 'O LORD, have mercy on me; heal me, for I have sinned against you'" (Psalm 41:4).

Christian's great passion in life at the moment is a European line of toys called Playmobile. He has a fort and a pirate ship and all sorts of things that take about ten hours to assemble. Our house rule is if you drag it out, you put it away. That works fairly well most of the time but didn't one Tuesday night. He had been playing by himself happily for an hour, and then he asked me to bake sugar cookies that he could decorate. I told him I'd love to do that once he had put his toys away.

"I can't! There are too many," he said.

"Well, you shouldn't have taken so many out," I told him. "You put them away, and then we'll make fantastic cookies."

"No!"

"Okay," I said. I went through to the bathroom to run his bath. He followed me in.

"What about my cookies?" he asked.

"I thought you decided we weren't making any," I answered.

"No, I didn't. You did," he said indignantly.

"No, Christian. I said that when you put your toys away, we would make cookies. You didn't put your toys away, so you voted for no cookies."

"That's not fair!" he said.

I see myself in my son so often. I'd love to blame everyone else in the world for my life and my choices, but I will never develop character and integrity until I take full responsibility for all my actions. It is our nature to shift the blame, but it is our calling to take full responsibility for our sins. There is great liberty and joy in God's ways when we submit to them. I wouldn't have believed that a few years ago; then I began to understand that there is no shame attached to honesty and truthfulness. Shame tells us we are bad people rather than sinners who make bad choices. Sinners like us will be forgiven by God when we confess our wrongs with a repentant heart.

REALITY

"And we rejoice in the hope of the glory of God. Not only so, but we also rejoice in our sufferings, because we know that suffering produces perseverance; perseverance, character; and character, hope. And hope does not disappoint us" (Romans 5:2-5).

"Nothing works!" I laugh every time I hear Luci Swindoll make this declaration, but there is a ring of truth to it. Life is inherently disappointing. Nothing is quite as great as it's made out to be. Children want things to be perfect. We all do. Nothing is. I will never be the perfect mother no matter how hard I try. I am a sinner. Part of my job in raising Christian is to help him understand the reality that neither life nor other people can ever be perfect. It's hard to see the look of disappointment on his face when a friend hurts him or his fish dies or the ice cream store is closed. But that's life, and part of developing character is learning to deal with it.

Sometimes we shade reality in an attempt to buffer ourselves from life's disappointments. Christian was sitting on the end of the bed watching a show on PBS. He was so into it that he didn't see how close he was to the edge until he fell off.

"Are you okay?" I asked.

"Mom, you pushed me off the bed!" he said.

I stared at him and said nothing. He started to laugh. I was at the other end of the room, writing on my computer, nowhere near him.

"All right, you didn't," he said with a sheepish grin.

Being loved helps us face the reality of life. We can be silly or disappointed or downright wrong without being shamed.

COMPETENCE

"And God is able to make all grace abound to you, so that in all things at all times, having all that you need, you will abound in every good work" (2 Corinthians 9:8).

Barry is an only child. His parents waited a long time for him. When he arrived, they wanted to make life as easy and happy for him as possible. That's not always the best gift to a child, however. When he went to college, Barry's parents would often drive up on weekends to do his laundry or clean his dorm room. In their hearts they wanted his life to be a bed of roses, but life is not like that, and we never develop character unless we learn to fail and get back up and try again.

When we as parents step in all the time rather than allow our children to make mistakes and learn from them, we do them a disservice. It can be frustrating, even terrifying at times, to sit back and watch when we know that what they are trying won't work, but how else will they learn?

I love the process of finding out what Christian is drawn to and encouraging that in him. He developed a love for ice skating, so we signed him up for lessons as soon as they opened an ice rink close to our house. It was so funny watching him and seven other four-year-olds shuffle about the ice and land on their bottoms more often than not.

After one big fall Christian came over to the edge of the ice where Barry and I were watching. He'd had enough.

"You're my favorite kind of skater," I told him.

He looked at me dubiously. "What do you mean?" he asked.

"When you fall down, you get back up and try again. That's my favorite kind of skater."

Now whenever he falls, he looks to see where we are, gives us a big thumbs-up, and carries on. But his lack of ability frustrates him. He wants to be a good hitter when we play baseball in the yard, but more often than not he misses the ball. One of the things Barry and I are working on with him is being a team player. Boys are so competitive, and that can be a good thing. But we're trying to help our son see the fun and pure joy of simply being a part of something, even if he doesn't win. We want him to understand most of all that he is lovable and loved, simply because he *is*. His competence as a human being doesn't lie in his natural abilities (or lack thereof) but in his inherent value to the God who created him.

CONSCIENCE

"The goal of this command is love, which comes from a pure heart and a good conscience and a sincere faith" (1 Timothy 1:5).

Conscience is a controversial subject these days. Some would liberate us from one entirely; others would have all joy robbed from life as our conscience takes on the voice of an ogre. Neither is healthy. A healthy conscience is like an internal radar that helps us to land on the right runway and also allows us to take responsibility when we don't so we can find the right path again.

One of my friends has a fourteen-year-old daughter. She asked her mom one Friday night if she could go to the movies with two of her school friends. My friend asked what movie they planned to see. Her daughter told her it was a PG-13 movie they had intended to see as a family anyway, so Mom said that would be fine.

One of the other girls' moms was going to drop them off, and my friend was going to pick them up after the movie was over. My friend showed up a bit early and saw her daughter sitting alone on the sidewalk outside the theater.

"Hi! What's up? Didn't you like the movie?" she asked.

"Mom, I lied to you. We went to an R-rated movie. After a while I felt so bad that I came out here to wait for you. I'm so sorry."

"I'm disappointed that you lied to me, honey," her mom said. "But I'm proud that you left the movie and told me the truth."

Having an intact conscience doesn't mean that a child will never make bad choices but rather that he or she will be aware of them and choose a different path. For all of us, no matter what age, keeping a clear conscience requires being able to tell the truth and ask forgiveness when we are wrong.

WORSHIP

"For you have been my hope, O Sovereign LORD, my confidence since my youth. From birth I have relied on you; you brought me forth from my mother's womb. I will ever praise you" (Psalm 71:5-6).

That is the greatest prayer of any Christian parent, that their children will love God from an early age. When I was pregnant, I had two specific prayers for the child in my womb. I prayed that he would have a compassionate heart and that he would find a meaningful relationship with God when he was young. I don't know how children make it through the harsh realities of life in the twenty-first century without a belief in the love and goodness of God. That's why I also prayed, "God, show me how to love my child in such a way that he will hunger to know you."

I love going a little bit early to pick up Christian from Sunday school. I don't go in; I just peek in the window. It is a beautiful sight to watch your child sing songs about the love of God, bow his head in prayer, and give thanks. It's wonderful to watch an independent relationship with God begin to grow.

On a recent Women of Faith trip I had stomach flu and was feeling very sorry for myself. Barry took Christian downstairs in the hotel to eat while I rested in bed. As they came back in after dinner, Christian tiptoed over to the side of the bed. "Come on, Dad," he said. As I lay there with my eyes closed, my son prayed for me. "Dear God, Mommy doesn't feel very good. Please make her better. I love her. Amen."

I couldn't have asked for a purer, more worshipful moment!

THE TRUTH ABOUT THIS LIFE

Jesus said, "Then you will know the truth, and the truth will set you free" (John 8:32). One of the hardest tasks of my life has been embracing what's true about me. I hear that same struggle in my friends. Every year at Women of Faith conferences we show a short video to introduce the speakers to the audience. One of the questions posed to us in the 2001 video was, "What do you find hard to accept about yourself?"

My answer was, "I find it much easier to be angry than to admit that I'm afraid."

Patsy Clairmont's answer was, "To accept the reflection in the mirror."

Marilyn Meberg said, "There is a little something wrong with everything about me!"

We are not alone in our struggle to face the truth about ourselves. The gift that we have to give our children, however, is that God's love is *so* big, so wide, so deep, so boundless that we can face what is true and not be consumed or condemned by it. Love, grace, and forgiveness enable us to take an honest look at all that is true about us and offer it up to God in return for unconditional love and supernatural transformation.

I love the writings of Frederick Buechner. I am drawn by his honesty and vulnerability. One of my favorite books is Buechner's *Telling the Truth: The Gospel as Tragedy, Comedy and Fairy Tale.* This text resonated loudly with me because for a long time I felt as if I was part of something that had the faint aroma of a sham. I didn't doubt the love or existence of God, but I doubted how we as believers, especially those of us in public ministry, were presenting him. Too often it sounded as if we were saying that if we just had enough faith, everything in life would turn out just as we hoped. Our children would love God, our health would defy all odds, and our finances would be as abundant as the waters over Niagara Falls. That's not reality. If we act as shifty PR agents for God, we sell something that will not sustain people when life inevitably becomes painful.

I will never cease to be amazed at the way God continues to use the worst moments of my life to bring hope to other people. Who but God could take the broken bridge of depression and use it to lead others out of darkness? I have come to believe passionately that we just *have* to tell the truth. Life is painful and hard to understand, and we do each other and our children and ourselves a disservice when we force smiles when tears would be more appropriate.

It is painful to watch my son grieve the loss of his papa. But his tears and sadness pay tribute to the love that William showered upon him for the first four years of his life. I don't pretend to have the answer to Christian's question "Why did God take my papa?" All I can do is hold my son and weep with him. As Buechner says to those of us who proclaim the gospel to others, "If he does not make real to them the human experience of what it is to cry into the storm and receive no answer, to be sick at heart and find no healing, then he becomes the only one there who seems not to have had that experience.... All the others there have had it whether they talk about it or not."

Buechner's assertion is not a fatalistic throwing up of hands in despair, however. He's simply saying that if we get rid of the myths and the lies and the facades, then there is finally room for the glorious truth. And that truth will set us free to shine like candles in the darkness.

Fear

A wonderful Savior is Jesus my Lord,
He taketh my burden away;
He holdeth me up, and I shall not be moved,
He giveth me strength for each day.

He hideth my soul in the cleft of the rock
That shadows a dry, thirsty land;
He hideth my life in the depths of His love,
And covers me there with His hand.

—Fanny J. Crosby, "He Hideth My Soul"

5

≡ FEAR ≡

A DISPLACED LOVE

Even though I walk through the valley of the shadow of death,
I will fear no evil, for you are with me;
your rod and your staff, they comfort me.

PSALM 23:4

There are such things as the treasures of darkness. The darkness, thank God,
passes. But what one learns in the darkness, one possesses forever.

LESLIE WETHERHEAD

I was in the kitchen fixing breakfast for Christian when I heard my assistant, Pat, calling my name. I went upstairs to the office. She sounded concerned. "Read this," she said.

She handed me a fax that had just come from my friend and fellow speaker Barbara Johnson. I read it. I read it again, trying to assimilate what I was reading. I couldn't believe it. Barbara had faxed me a copy of a card she'd received in the mail the day before. It said:

Congratulations that the Lord is calling you home.
You have expressed your love for your boys, and now the time is
    coming to be with them.
Remember, instant death, instant glory!

We will miss you as a part of the Women of Faith team, but
where you are going is an honor to be part of an eternal
team.

My mind went back to a phone call I'd received two months earlier
from Mary Graham, president of Women of Faith. "I have some bad
news, Sheila. Barb has a brain tumor."

"What do you mean?" I said, stunned. "We were just together. She
seemed fine."

"I know, but she had a little tumble the other day and couldn't get
up. Her doctor ordered an MRI, and that's how the tumor was discovered. She will have surgery tomorrow."

I was supposed to be leaving for Dallas the next morning to be on a
television show, but I wanted to be with Barbara. I talked to Barry, and
we agreed that I should cancel the show and fly out first thing in the
morning. That night I lay in bed with tears streaming down my cheeks
and questions pouring over my soul. "Why Barbara, Lord? Hasn't she
had more than enough already?"

Barbara Johnson has buried two sons, lost contact with one son for
eleven years, and nursed her husband through a horrific car accident
that he was not expected to survive. At one time her despair brought her
to the edge of suicide as she contemplated driving her car off the edge
of a viaduct close to her home in Southern California. At that blackest
moment Barbara remembered who she is: a beloved child of God. And
she prayed a simple, profound prayer of absolute surrender: "Whatever,
Lord. Whatever you bring into my life, I will love and serve you." From
that moment when her life was brought back from the edge to this
moment, God has used her to bring hope and healing to thousands of
parents all over the world. Her tears have watered dried-out hearts, and
the fragrance of her life has brought a sweet perfume to bitter places.
Now this! How much more could one person bear?

I arrived at the airport in Orange County, California, the following day two hours before Barb's surgery was to begin. In my haste to change my travel plans, I hadn't thought to call ahead for a rental car, but I wasn't too concerned. There are always cars available at that airport. I had quite a bit of luggage with me, as I was going to fly from there to the next Women of Faith conference. I grabbed my bags and hauled them like dead carcasses over to the car rental area. At every counter I was assaulted by signs stating, "No Cars Available." I asked the man behind one of the desks what was going on.

"There is an optometrists convention going on in Anaheim. There are thousands of them! You won't find a car for miles, but you can sure get your eyes tested!"

I was not amused. I needed a car. I couldn't get a cab and drag all my bags into the hospital with me. "Lord, I need some help here. I need a car. Any old car will do. Any color will do. I'll drive a plaid Yugo. I just need a car."

The young comedian who had told me there was no hope of finding a car called me over. "Do you really need a car?" he asked.

"Yes! I really need a car," I assured him.

"Go outside and wait for five minutes. A large man will pick you up in a small red van."

"Is there any special handshake?" I asked, trying to enter his world of pithy quips.

"No," he said. I guess his humor was a passing thing.

In normal circumstances I would not go outside and wait for a large man in a small red van or a small man in a large red van, but these were not normal circumstances. I waited, and sure enough, five minutes later, a small red van pulled up. I got in, and the driver took me to an off-site car rental office.

"We have one car left," he said.

"I'll take it." I gave him my credit-card imprint and my left kidney, threw my bags in the trunk, and headed for St. Jude's Hospital in Fullerton. I called Mary Graham from the car. She was at the hospital already and told me to take the first elevator when I came in through the main doors. I found a bank of elevators and pressed the button for the fifth floor. I emerged into a lovely, bright, cheerful nurses' station.

"Can you tell me what room Barbara Johnson is in?" I asked.

"Well certainly," a perky nurse said. "Is it a boy or a girl?"

I looked at her as if she had lost her marbles. "Well, I guess she's a girl, but she's in her seventies," I said.

The nurse looked at me as if my marbles had escaped with her marbles. "Is she the grandmother?"

"Yes, she's a grandmother. What does that have to do with her brain tumor?" I asked.

"Ma'am, this is the maternity wing. You took the wrong elevator."

I exited as quickly as I could, muttering something about being a stranger in this country, and finally found Barb's room. She was sitting up in bed, laughing at something Mary had said. I hugged her, and we talked for a while until the nurse came to get her ready for surgery.

"Are you afraid, Barb?" I asked.

"No, I'm not afraid. God has been faithful to me too many times for me to be afraid."

She was in surgery for six hours. Mary and I waited with her family. We told each other our favorite Barbara stories. Finally the surgeon came back to the waiting room.

"Well, the surgery was a success," he said. "She is doing well. The tumor is malignant, but it's treatable. I couldn't take it out. It's positioned in a place that I don't want to interfere with. The good news is that this kind of cancer responds well to chemotherapy." Barbara's husband, Bill, put his head in his hands. It was an overwhelming moment.

We came back the next morning, but I didn't expect to be able to see Barb, as the hospital allows only family in the intensive care unit. But, as usual, Barbara had thought of everything. She had put Mary and me down on the list at the nurses' station as her daughters!

It was a shock to see Barb for the first time after surgery. Her hair was shaved, and she was cut from ear to ear over the top of her head. Large staples marked her scalp every half-inch, holding the incision closed. I bent over to kiss her sweet face. She was awake and alert.

"The doctor told me last night that I was about to face the most difficult twenty-four hours of my life as I got used to the news that I have cancer," she said. "I just laughed and told him, 'You obviously don't know much about my life!'"

Three days later she was released and began a ten-week program of chemotherapy. She was halfway through her treatment when she received the note she faxed to me: "Congratulations that the Lord is calling you home...."

I looked at the signature and telephone number at the bottom of the note. I didn't recognize the name. I called Barbara. "I got your fax. What is that all about?" I asked.

"Isn't that something!" she said with a chuckle. "Do you think I should have myself measured for a casket?" Barbara had no idea who the woman was who had sent her the card. She was taking it lightly, but it made me mad that someone would send a note like that to her when she was weak and sick from the chemo. When I got off the phone, I tracked the number to a small town in Oregon and called. The woman who wrote the note answered the phone. I told her who I was and asked her why she'd sent it.

"Well, I heard Barbara has less than six months to live, so I was trying to help her. I didn't want her to be afraid. I thought my note would prepare her."

Prepare her for what? I thought. *A coma?!*

After we talked for a while, it became clear to me that this woman had heard an erroneous rumor that Barbara's cancer was inoperable and that she was dying. The woman had heard that Barbara was being consumed with fear, and she wanted to help. She wanted Barb to think of the joy of being reunited with her sons.

Speaking for myself, receiving my own death notice in the mail would not cheer me up. Cookies might do it, flowers perhaps, but not the old "Your time's up!" approach.

LIFE IS SCARY

Fear. It is part of all our lives. For some of us it occupies a large percentage of the property of our souls; for others it fights for space and is relegated to the back room somewhere. Barbara is like that. Fear is there; it just doesn't get much room. She has a history of facing the unthinkable and has found God to be faithful in every circumstance.

I like to watch children on the playground. Some fly like monkeys across bars, leap off blocks, and careen around like two-legged windmills. Others play it safe. They watch. They get out of the way. They envision dangers that haven't materialized yet. They are careful and clean. Is that a learned behavior or a caution built into their genes? Why do some children have nightmares that terrorize their sleep and others see nothing in the night but the pale reflection of the silver moon on their pillows? I think some children are naturally timid. I also think that life can teach you too soon that there is more over the rainbow than lemon drops.

Barry and I have both struggled with fear. As a child I went from the whirling dervish type to the timid flip side almost overnight. Children cannot process violence and death well. My father's brain hemorrhage, personality change, and subsequent death were a dark and confusing melodrama to me. Barry grew up with parents who were afraid of what might happen. This left a legacy of uncertainty and fear inside him. It robbed him of some of the joy of what was good as he worried about what might change for the worse at any moment.

We don't want to pass our fears on to our child. Fear is an inevitable part of living as a human being in this world. We can't completely escape being afraid. But fear doesn't have to take over our lives and spoil God's party in our souls.

"Where are you going, Mom?" Christian asks.

"I'm just going to the rest room, darling," I say.

"I'll wait outside."

I have an extra limb now. Christian has adopted the spirit of Ruth. "Wherever thou goest I will go. Thy bathroom shall be my bathroom and thy lunch, my lunch." He won't let me out of his sight. I am supposed to go to India for a week. I cancel the trip. He sits so close to me it's as if he's trying to burrow under my skin and hide inside. I understand. We followed the ambulance carrying his papa to the hospital. We came home alone. At first he cried a lot. Then he was quiet and sad. Every time I get up to go into the kitchen or the bathroom, he follows. It's as if he's decided that nothing bad can happen to me if he stays close. He stays very close.

"Where is Papa?" he asks.

"Papa is in heaven," I say.

"Where is that?"

"Papa is safe with Jesus," I answer, struggling for words.

"But I want him here. I didn't want him to go. He never said good-bye."

He won't sleep alone now. Barry and I moved a mattress into his room so we could take turns helping him through the terror of night, when the unthinkable seems thinkable. How can I help him? What can I tuck into his young soul that will last through a lifetime of fears, real and imagined?

I remember Patsy Clairmont's telling me a story about when her boy, Jason, was little, and I comb it in my mind for some help. Jason was the loser in a wrestling match with his big brother, Marty. He was catapulted through the air and landed against the edge of a wall, splitting his head open. On the way to the hospital he asked his mom what they were going to do to him.

"They're going to put you back together again," she said, hoping he'd leave it there. Children never leave it there.

"Well, how will they do that?" he pressed.

"They'll make it meet in the middle again," she offered.

"How will they do that?" he probed.

"They're going to have to stitch that puppy shut!" she said.

"What will I do if it gets too much to bear?" Jason asked with the terrified look of the proverbial deer caught in the headlights.

"You're going to ask Jesus to help you reach down inside and grab your courage and pull it up!"

As they were driving home after Jason's wound was stitched up, a pale-faced Patsy asked her son if it had ever become so hard to bear that he'd had to ask Jesus for help.

"I didn't wait for that, Mom. As soon as you told me, I asked Jesus for help there and then."

That's a good way to live. Don't wait until it's too much to bear.

I can't tell Christian that bad things won't happen. He already knows that they do. I can't tell him that if he loves God, he will never be afraid. I don't believe that.

I can tell him that he will never be alone.

I can tell him that even in the darkest night, God will be there with him.

I can tell him that because Christ faced abandonment and desolation on our behalf, he will never be abandoned.

I can tell him that with every experience in which he puts his hand in God's hand, fear will have a smaller voice.

I can tell him that he can tell me anything.

I can tell him that he can tell God anything.

I can tell him that fear doesn't seem so huge when you share it with a trusted Friend.

THE TRAIL OF GOD'S FAITHFULNESS

"Come on, Son. We'd better start early. It's going to be a long day."

The father had been up early, chopping enough wood for the trip. They traveled for three days, and then he saw it in the distance. He knew that this was the right place. He said to his servants, "Stay here. The boy and I will go on alone. We'll be back."

"Dad, where's the animal for the sacrifice?"

"God will provide it. Don't worry," he told Isaac.

I can't imagine what those days were like for Abraham. He had waited a long time for this boy. God had promised that through Isaac, Abraham's only son, God would make his descendants as numerous as the stars in the sky. Then God had said, "Take your son and sacrifice him to me." Abraham got up and with his own hands chopped the wood that would consume his son. He had no idea where they were going when they set out. God had told him, "I'll show you the place. Just start." So they began.

They began. That simple act of beginning is full of meaning. Abraham had no idea how everything would unfold. All he knew was that a father's greatest nightmare waited for him at the end of his journey. Yet he took the first step, and the next.

There are several more amazing things about this story recorded in Genesis 22. Abraham told the servants that he and Isaac would be back. How did he know that? The text makes it clear that Abraham had no intention of holding back his son. He asked Isaac to carry the wood, just as later One much greater than he would carry the wood on which his human life would be extinguished as the ultimate sacrifice for us all. Abraham told the servants that Isaac and he were going to worship.

What an interesting word to use! He was going up a mountain with a knife and with his precious son, but in his heart he was going to worship. That is a significant key to living a life that is not consumed by fear: to see all of life as worship. C. S. Lewis wrote, "We take steps with God and at every step offer our lives as worship. In the process of worshipping God he communicates his Spirit to us." If we viewed every moment as an act of worshiping God, how would it change the landscape of our minds and souls?

This was not Abraham's first encounter with the peculiar ways of God. When he was seventy-five years old, God told him to leave his land and go to a place God would show him. Abraham went, taking his family, and left all that was sure and safe. He had no idea where he was going, but he packed up his family and his nephew, Lot, and followed God. Then God told him to separate from Lot, his closest family member. Abraham did it. In his passivity about which direction to take, Abraham almost gave Lot the Promised Land. But Lot chose the land that looked good to him at the moment, and he later became the father of the Ammonites and the Moabites, the people throughout Israel's subsequent history who were the primary obstacle to the fulfillment of God's promise to Abraham.

In all these things, Abraham saw the hand of God. So when God said, "Take the boy," Abraham did not question God. I believe he thought, *Even if I have to kill Isaac, God can raise him from the dead.* Abraham kept his heart focused on God rather than on what God had told him to do.

There is a huge lesson here for me and perhaps for you. I am more consumed at times by what I think God should do than who he is. If I focused more on who he is than on the events unfolding before my eyes, I believe I would be much less afraid. Abraham was known as God's friend, someone God would talk to. God asked difficult things of Abraham, and Abraham obeyed, no matter how impossible things seemed. And God proved faithful. "By faith Abraham, even though he was past age—and Sarah herself was barren—was enabled to become a father because he considered him faithful who had made the promise. And so from this one man, and he as good as dead, came descendants as numerous as the stars in the sky and as countless as the sand on the seashore" (Hebrews 11:11-12).

So even though I can't promise my child that he will never be afraid, I can point to the faithful ways of God. This is the key. Life can be full of unexpected twists and turns, but God will meet us at every single one of them.

"FEAR NOT"

This is the familiar greeting of angels. It's like a mandate, a command. I wonder if they speak to the person who houses the fear ("Do not fear!") or to the fear itself ("Fear! You are not welcome here. You don't belong. God is here. You have to go!").

Scripture testifies to the truth that the fear of the Lord is the beginning of all wisdom. Fear in that context is the awe and reverence that is appropriate from sinful mortal men and women toward God, who is altogether holy and good. In our contemporary culture it seems we have exchanged that holy fear for the terror of life. It is a poor substitute. I believe that the more space we make in our lives for a deep and holy reverence for God, the less room there will be for the kind of fear that cripples us.

If we fear God, we fear nothing else. If we don't fear God, we fear everything else. A reverent fear of God assures us that although anything might happen, it has passed through the merciful hands of a loving Father, and we will never be alone or abandoned.

In the process of writing *Living Fearlessly,* I realized that what I most deeply needed was not to become more courageous but to know God better. And that is what I want to live out before my son. I am very grateful as I look back at the way my mother lived out her life before my brother, sister, and me. As an adult I understand that there were many times when she made barely enough money to survive, but as a child I never knew that. My mother trusted God. She knew that God was our provider. As a result of her faith, we felt safe and secure.

Remember when the disciples were together in the Upper Room after the Crucifixion? They were terrified. They were lost. They were leaderless. Christ was dead, and they were alone. Then the risen Christ appeared to them and said, "Peace. Be still." Nothing else had changed. The crowds were still outside the door. The Romans were still in charge. But Jesus was there, so everything had changed.

That is our great hope and promise today and every day. Christ is here, so everything has changed. Perhaps your life seems out of control at the moment, and you're overwhelmed by the circumstances that bark at your heels. You are not alone. Your children are not alone. The risen Christ is here. Take your life to him and worship.

LIVING FEARLESSLY

When I was fourteen, Carol Woods was the bane of my life. She took great delight in tormenting me daily. Her favorite thing was to hold me on the school bus past my stop. It sounds like such a small thing now, but it cast a shadow over my whole day. Hours before it was time to go home, I would try to think of ways I could avoid her. I'm sure she gave me little thought until she would see me trying to appear invisible in the line as we got on the school bus. Some afternoons I would let the bus go and walk the five miles home rather than face what might happen.

I have had a Carol Woods in my life on occasion even as an adult. The scenario is always the same. I perceive the person to be more powerful than I am, with the ability to harm me. After I was released from the psychiatric unit, I faced more Carol Woodses in the form of those who challenged whether a Christian should ever be hospitalized for depression. I remember receiving a call one evening from a friend I hadn't talked to in some time. She was horrified that I had "lost faith," as she perceived it.

After I got off the phone, I sat on the floor in the dark for a while, tears pouring down my cheeks. Suddenly, by the light of the fire, I caught a glimpse of myself in the mirror, and it was a real wake-up call. I looked as if I were five years old, huddled up tight, trying to keep the bogeyman away. I stood up, turned on the light, and talked to myself. "Sheila, how long are you going to allow other people to shame you and rob you of joy and peace? Stop this now! God loves you. He is still on the throne. If God is through with you, you're through, but if not, you're not. And no matter what, he's promised that nothing can separate you from his love."

I began that night to replace all the lies and tapes that were so old they were eight-tracks playing in my head. I began to replace them with what is true. "For I am convinced that neither death nor life, neither angels nor demons, neither the present nor the future, nor any powers, neither height nor depth, nor anything else in all creation, will be able to separate us from the love of God that is in Christ Jesus our Lord" (Romans 8:38-39). I began to read the Bible out loud. We are sensory creatures, and there is power in letting our ears hear what our mind is taking in. That's how the psalms were used—during communal worship. I began to write verses down on Post-it notes and put them where I would see them often: on the refrigerator, in my car, on the bathroom mirror. And I would read them aloud, over and over.

> The LORD is my light and my salvation—
>   whom shall I fear?
> The LORD is the stronghold of my life—
>   of whom shall I be afraid? (Psalm 27:1)

It took a lot to free me from the fear of those I perceived as more powerful than I. The psalmist David helped me most, along with a little book by Gene Edwards called *A Tale of Three Kings* about Saul, David, and Absalom. It is a story about those who attempt to wield power in the name of the Lord and wound those around them as a result. It is a story of those who thrive on instilling fear in others and those who flourish because of their passionate belief in the love and goodness of God.

Remember the day that David was pulled from his job in the fields as a shepherd boy? He was brought before the prophet Samuel. When Samuel saw the young boy, God said to him, "Rise and anoint him; he is the one." We all long to be "the one." We want to feel special, chosen, cherished. But what David was inducted into that day was ten years of brokenness and terror at the hands of a mad king.

The first time Saul met David, he liked him and requested that he stay with him in the palace as an armorbearer. Saul was an internally tormented man, and often David comforted him by singing songs and playing instruments, but Saul saw in this young man a rival. David was clearly gifted and anointed by God, and this consumed Saul with jealousy. (Fear left unattended can simmer into a jealous rage.) Saul determined that he was going to kill David, so David ran and hid in a cave.

Dark days. David didn't know that they were the very days that were preparing him to become king of Israel. Only God knew that. Out of his brokenness and pain, David, through his writings and songs, became the greatest spokesperson of all time for the anguish of the human soul and the comfort to be found in God alone. David could never have imagined that thousands of years later you and I would turn to his psalms to give words to the fears and questions in our hearts as we have sat in our own caves and dark places.

When he was thirty years old, David became the shepherd king of Israel, a foreshadowing of Christ, our Shepherd King, who came directly from David's lineage. I look at the way David refused to be like Saul, and I am amazed, but I look at the way David treated Absalom, his own son, and I am silenced. David was used to having spears thrown at him by King Saul. God protected David, and he never threw one back. But how would you protect yourself from your own son if you became king and he decided to get rid of you and split God's kingdom in two? What would you do?

When David was warned that his third son, the handsomest man in Israel, was plotting his death, David decided to do nothing. At first this is hard to understand. David was God's chosen king. If Absalom took over, he was not the one God had chosen, and he threatened to divide the kingdom. Wasn't it David's job to defend what God had put together? David believed that his life was in God's hands, not Absalom's. This was David's response: "Let him do to me whatever seems good to him" (2 Samuel 15:26). What a reply! He was saying, "If God is through with me, then I am through. If he is not, then I am not."

What a revolutionary way to live. When you feel threatened, when someone else intends to harm you, how do you respond? Do you act out of the holy fear of God or the terrified fear of man? For years I lived out of the fear of what man or woman could do to me. Now I believe with my whole heart that my life is in God's hands.

"Who are you that you fear mortal men, the sons of men, who are but grass, that you forget the LORD your Maker, who stretched out the heavens and laid the foundations of the earth, that you live in constant terror every day because of the wrath of the oppressor, who is bent on destruction? For where is the wrath of the oppressor?...For I am the LORD your God" (Isaiah 51:12-13,15).

When we make God our defender, our confidence is in his love. So how do we live before our children in a way that models total confidence in his goodness and love in a world that perceives that stance as weakness or head-in-the-sand blindness? How do we model total confidence in God's goodness and love in a world that is full of evil?

I dropped Christian off at school, and as I was getting back into my car, I saw a boy slap him hard even though Christian wasn't doing anything. The boy's mother watched and said nothing. In my heart

I wanted to slap her and ship her child off to Bosnia. Christian and I talked about it that night.

"Why did he do that, Mom?"

"I don't know, babe," I said. "Perhaps he's got stuff going on inside him that he can't handle. Do you want to pray for him?" I asked.

"No way!" he replied.

"May I?"

"If you want to," he said, obviously unimpressed with his godly mother.

"Father God, thank you so much for Christian. Thank you that you chose me to be his mommy. I want to ask you about Alex. I've no idea why he hit Christian. Christian didn't deserve it. You know what that's like. You paid for all our stuff, and you didn't deserve it. Help Alex to find a way to talk about what's going on inside of him without hitting others. Help Christian to forgive him. Amen."

Do I tell my boy to stand by for the rest of his life and let others hit him? No, I don't want to do that. I tell him he can walk away. I tell him if someone persists in hitting him, he can warn him, and then he can defend himself. Am I right in my counsel? I don't know. What I do know is that I don't want my son to be afraid. I don't want his love to be displaced. I want his confidence to be built firmly on his trust in the love of God, not in his own ability to wield power. I want him to fear God, not people. I want him to taste the astonishingly humble confidence of Jesus Christ. "He was oppressed and afflicted, yet he did not open his mouth; he was led like a lamb to the slaughter, and as a sheep before her shearers is silent, so he did not open his mouth" (Isaiah 53:7).

EAGLE'S WINGS

"My husband lost his job last week," she began. "I don't know what we're going to do. We could lose our house. What do I say to the children? I am so afraid!"

I looked into the eyes of this woman in her thirties who had stood in line for over an hour to cast her net into the well of my soul, hoping to catch something that would help her make it through.

How do you handle something like that? How do you hide the fear that is tearing at you? Perhaps for as long as you can remember, you have been a patchwork quilt of fears. Perhaps the quilt is a family heirloom, passed on from generation to generation.

I believe that God can help you make a new quilt. David proclaimed, "My flesh and my heart may fail, but God is the strength of my heart and my portion forever" (Psalm 73:26).

Isaiah recorded:

"To whom will you compare me?
    Or who is my equal?" says the Holy One.
Lift your eyes and look to the heavens:
    Who created all these?
He who brings out the starry host one by one,
    and calls them each by name.
Because of his great power and mighty strength,
    not one of them is missing.

Why do you say, O Jacob,
    and complain, O Israel,
"My way is hidden from the LORD;
    my cause is disregarded by my God"?
Do you not know?
    Have you not heard?
The LORD is the everlasting God,
    the Creator of the ends of the earth.
He will not grow tired or weary,
    and his understanding no one can fathom.
He gives strength to the weary
    and increases the power of the weak.

Even youths grow tired and weary,
   and young men stumble and fall;
but those who hope in the LORD
   will renew their strength.
They will soar on wings like eagles;
   they will run and not grow weary,
   they will walk and not be faint. (Isaiah 40:25-31)

The eagle is an awesome bird. It has a massive wingspan and is one of the most powerful birds known to modern man. An adult eagle eats over five hundred pounds of food every year—not a cost-effective pet!

Despite its power, however, the eagle is dependent on the wind. That is one of the reasons eagles' nests are always high on a cliff: The eagle needs the updraft of the wind to fly. When a mother eagle decides that it's time for her young ones to fly, she pushes them out of the nest and watches to see what they'll do. If they fly, she lets them fly. If they begin to fall, she swoops down under them, catches them on her wings, and places them back safely in the nest. She continues to do this until they can fly on their own.

I accept that fear is a part of life. I also know that God is everywhere. I know that his love and grace are always available in abundance. I know that his forgiveness and mercy will enable me to embrace what is true, even the fact that flying is scary.

We're not asked to fly on our own; we are just asked to trust the master eagle. When he pushes us out of the nest, we can dare to stretch out our wings and let the wind of the Holy Spirit carry us. We fly, and then we teach our children to do the same.

Anger

May the mind of Christ, my Savior,
Live in me from day to day,
By His love and power controlling
All I do and say.

May the word of God dwell richly
In my heart from hour to hour,
So that all may see I triumph
Only through His power.

—Kate B. Wilkinson, "May the Mind
of Christ, My Savior"

6

≡ ANGER ≡

A BRUISED LOVE

In your anger do not sin;
when you are on your beds,
search your hearts and be silent.

PSALM 4:4

Unholy tempers are always unhappy tempers.

JOHN WESLEY

The noise in the temple court that day was deafening. It was more than he could bear. He had been here many times before. He had been brought here first by his parents when he was a tiny baby. That first trip was special, his mother would often say. It was special for the old man who was waiting there; special for her, too. She would retell the story of the look in Simeon's eyes when he saw her precious boy and the prayer he prayed as he held him in his arms. "Sovereign Lord, as you have promised, you now dismiss your servant in peace. For my eyes have seen your salvation, which you have prepared in the sight of all people, a light for revelation to the Gentiles and for glory to your people Israel" (Luke 2:29-32).

"What did he mean, Mother?" he would ask her. "What did he see?"

But Mary would simply smile and get that faraway look in her eyes. That look was as familiar to him as the bread she baked every morning.

Then there was the time when he had stayed behind at the temple to talk and debate with the teachers. He had felt so alive that day, so at home. His mother thought he was with their group returning home. She had been very cross when she found him.

"We thought you were lost. Don't ever do that again!" she had scolded.

"But I have to be in my Father's house," he said. They didn't understand.

Then there was that bleak day when he was at his weakest. His enemy knew that of course. He had taken him here, to the tallest point of the temple. "'If you are the Son of God,' he said, 'throw yourself down. For it is written: "He will command his angels concerning you, and they will lift you up in their hands, so that you will not strike your foot against a stone"'" (Matthew 4:6).

His enemy knew God's Word. He quoted it well, for indeed that was what the psalmist David had said. Jesus was told, "I'll give you it all without the pain, without the suffering. I can give you everything now." He had said no.

He had gone on to teach within these temple courts. He had sent the blind away with a new world stretched out in glorious color before them, eyes clear and bright, filled with wonder. He had sent the lame away amazed and dancing. But this! This was too much.

The temple courtyard was heaving with people. He looked into the eyes of the poor who had traveled miles to make a sacrifice. The sacrifice told in their clothes, their thin frames and sallow complexions. He looked into the greedy, lust-filled eyes of those who sold their wares at prices beyond the poor. This was his Father's house, and they had turned it into a black market, a cesspool of thieves and leeches. This was the second time he had disrupted their enterprises, and he was angry.

He turned over the tables and sent birds flying, money scattering in the dust, oil for sacrifices mixing with the dry sand. He grabbed a whip and began to chase those who groveled in the dirt, trying to rescue their money and their livestock. " 'It is written,' he said to them, ' "My house will be called a house of prayer," but you are making it a "den of robbers" ' " (Matthew 21:13). He was consumed with righteous rage for the purity and purpose of his Father's house.

When Jesus surveyed the scene, he saw this sacred place of worship, prayer, and praise filled with the noise of bleating animals and greedy men shouting to be heard above one another. He saw the people as sheep without a shepherd, abused and taken advantage of, all in the name of his Father. It was obscene, and he drove the greedy hordes into the streets.

His friends looked at him, amazed, as they remembered David's words: "I am a stranger to my brothers, an alien to my own mother's sons; for zeal for your house consumes me, and the insults of those who insult you fall on me" (Psalm 69:8-9).

Righteous rage. Christ showed anger for the right thing against the wrong thing. He left an example of what it looks like to be angry without sinning. That's my dilemma right there. I've got the anger bit down pat, but the "do not sin" part often eludes me. Of all the emotions I am challenged by, anger is my Achilles heel.

IT'S A BOMB!

Christian and I were playing our guessing game during bath time one evening.

"Can you tell me the name of an animal beginning with the letter *B?*" I asked.

"Buffalo!" he said.

"Good. Can you tell me the name of a bird beginning with the letter *H?*"

"Hostrich!" he shouted with glee.

"It's ostrich," I said laughing. "Not hostrich. The *h* shouldn't be there."

"Well, where will I put it then?" he asked.

Good question. Where will we put it—the anger inside us? If we bury it, we will end up sick in body or in mind with a monster in the basement of our souls. If we let it rip, we'll wound others as we fall into the darker pit of our lives. "Reckless words pierce like a sword" (Proverbs 12:18).

When I was in the psychiatric hospital, I was amused by the fact that there was an "Angry Room." It reminded me of the joke about two nuns driving through Transylvania. Suddenly Dracula jumped out in front of the car.

"Show him your cross!" one nun cried to the other.

The nun leaned out of the window and said, "I'm very, very cross!"

"What does one do in the angry room?" I inquired of my psychiatrist. "Does one just sit and be very, very cross?"

My sarcasm wasn't lost on my doctor.

"You might benefit from it, Sheila," he said with gentle firmness. "It's a safe place to get rid of all the stuff we carry inside without hurting anyone else." It was a Forrest Gump thing. It was a place to yell and scream if I needed to so that I could then lie at the foot of the cross and weep out the pain of my bruised soul. Anger doesn't need to be buried; it needs to be let go of. It needs to be lanced; it needs to be prayed out.

The psalms are a prime example of how that is done. Many scholars have a hard time with certain psalms, Psalm 137 in particular. It was popularized in Britain by a pop music group whose first hit was "By the Rivers of Babylon."

By the rivers of Babylon we sat and wept
    when we remembered Zion.
There on the poplars
    we hung our harps,

for there our captors asked us for songs,
> our tormentors demanded songs of joy;
> they said, "Sing us one of the songs of Zion!" (Psalm 137:1-3)

The psalm is a lament for God's people who have lost their home-land. In response to their captors' asking them to sing one of the songs of Zion, they refuse. They hang their instruments on the branches of trees. "How can we sing the songs of the LORD while in a foreign land?" (verse 4).

The text moves from this beautiful, poetic lament to a stanza of un-bridled hate. There's no other way to read it. "O Daughter of Babylon, doomed to destruction, happy is he who repays you for what you have done to us—he who seizes your infants and dashes them against the rocks" (verses 8-9).

It's interesting to note how many prayer books and hymnbooks have removed this stanza from their text. It offends with its raw malev-olence. The Hebrew word used for *happy* is the same word used in Psalm 1:1-2—*ashray*. "Blessed is the man who does not walk in the counsel of the wicked or stand in the way of sinners or sit in the seat of mockers. But his *delight* is in the law of the LORD, and on his law he meditates day and night."

Interesting to compare the delight in God's Word with the delight at seeing infants smashed against stones. But the spiteful words in Psalm 137 are there for a purpose. Eugene Peterson explains in his book *Answering God:* "Our hate needs to be prayed, not suppressed." That kind of hate is a response to the evil that exists in our world. I think back to Simon Wiesenthal's *The Sunflower* and the indictments of some of the Jewish writers who question the evangelical Christian's rush to for-give the most heinous evil. I have been challenged by their comments. Evil is real. I don't want to lose my sense of outrage at the injustice and horror that has become so commonplace in our world; I just need to know what to do with my anger and fear.

THERE IS A SOLUTION

Do not fret because of evil men
    or be envious of those who do wrong;
for like the grass they will soon wither,
    like green plants they will soon die away.

Trust in the LORD and do good;
    dwell in the land and enjoy safe pasture.
Delight yourself in the LORD
    and he will give you the desires of your heart.

Commit your way to the LORD;
    trust in him and he will do this:
He will make your righteousness shine like the dawn,
    the justice of your cause like the noonday sun.

Be still before the LORD and wait patiently for him;
    do not fret when men succeed in their ways,
    when they carry out their wicked schemes.
Refrain from anger and turn from wrath;
    do not fret—it leads only to evil. (Psalm 37:1-8)

God's anger as expressed over and over in the Old Testament is perfect. It is anger against evil. It is anger without fear. It is anger that seeks redemption and restoration rather than devastation and destruction. One of many examples of divine anger is recounted in the book of Jonah. God instructed this reluctant prophet to go preach to the people of Nineveh, warning them that he was going to destroy them for their wickedness, their pride, and their cruelty if they did not repent. Nineveh was a large city that dated back to the days just after the Flood

(Genesis 10:11). Jonah didn't want to go. He ran from his assignment and boarded a ship for Tarshish. "Then the LORD sent a great wind on the sea, and such a violent storm arose that the ship threatened to break up" (Jonah 1:4).

It's probable that all the sailors were Phoenician polytheists. To them, the number of prayers going up would matter, and the issue of not being sure which god was angry would enter into their reason for waking the sleeping Jonah to pray. "Pray to your favorite god till we can work out who has crossed whom. Maybe your god will save us!"

Jonah realized immediately what was happening and urged the sailors to throw him overboard to spare themselves. At first they were reluctant, but as the storm intensified, they tossed the prophet into the water, and the raging sea grew calm. Jonah was immediately gulped down by a great fish, which the story indicates was provided by the Lord himself. Some people dismiss this whole book as fable because, they reason, no one could survive in a fish belly for three days. But there is actually significant scientific evidence to the contrary. From inside the fish's stomach Jonah cried out to God in repentance and praise, and he was vomited onto dry land. He immediately set off on his original mission.

How did Jonah get God's message out to such a large crowd, probably about 120,000 people? His appearance was no doubt alarming. Anyone who had survived time inside the belly of a fish would be significantly marked on all exposed areas of his body by the stomach acid of the creature. But news of God's warning to the Ninevites spread like wildfire, and the people repented. God was angry at evil, expressed his anger, and accepted repentant hearts. "When God saw what they did and how they turned from their evil ways, he had compassion and did not bring upon them the destruction he had threatened" (Jonah 3:10). God's anger is perfect. And, of course, mine is not.

Not only do I deal with rage within myself, but I have also struggled for years to know how to deal with angry people and not be controlled by them. In the past when someone became angry with me, I lost all sense of what was right and what was wrong; all that motivated me at that point was how I could stop the anger. I lost all boundaries and reason and became like a child again.

If you recognize yourself in this scenario, it's likely that you experienced anger in your family when you were a child, as I did. In your reaction you go back to the dependency of a child who still lives with an angry person inside her head. You either cower or combust, depending on how you've habitually handled the anger and fear inside. In their best-selling book *Boundaries,* Drs. Henry Cloud and John Townsend suggest some ways to begin to deal with this.

REALIZE THAT IT'S A PROBLEM

This sounds simple, but owning up to what is true about oneself is a challenging and difficult process. For years I saw my problems as outside of myself. "I am this way because of such and such a person." That is never true. I am the way I am for many reasons, but it is up to me through the power of the Holy Spirit to change. No one can bring out of me what is not in me already, and I am always responsible for my response. I hate that! But it remains true whether I like it or not.

It is really good news wrapped in an unappealing package. If it were not true, then I would be a victim of everyone around me. But if I can take that first step of admitting there is a problem within *me,* then I have begun the process of positive and empowering change.

TALK TO SOMEONE; YOU WILL NOT WORK THIS OUT ALONE

Barry is a wonderful ally for me as I own this problem. He helps me see where I cross the line between reasonable debate and inappropriate venom. He is a very good snake handler! I love the way he is able to tell me when something I've said is unacceptable and yet maintains his love for me in the midst of it.

I have also benefited and continue to benefit from the input of trained, godly counselors. Shadows are not so dark and burdens are not so heavy when they are shared.

In the Context of These Supportive Relationships, Find the Source of the Fear

I discovered that my fear of a certain person in my life when I was in my thirties was really my fear of my father when I was three. The terror I felt when this person was angry with me was out of proportion to what was actually being said. All I knew was that I felt terror, I felt unsafe, and I wanted to run and hide.

When Barry and I were dating, he would react very strongly at times to things I said that he interpreted as my pulling away from him. When we talked, he discovered that even though the words came lightly out of my lips, he heard the weight of his mother's fears and anger in every word I said. It helps to put a face to the angry voice inside your head so you recognize its true source.

Talk Out the Hurts and Fears Regarding These Past Issues

I was thirty-four before I began to grieve the loss of my dad. I grieved the loss of his presence, the loss of aspects of my childhood. I grieved for my dad that such a terrible thing as a brain aneurysm happened to a young man with three little children.

Nicole Johnson describes a powerful scene in the movie *Forrest Gump*, where Jenny goes back to her childhood home. She stands outside looking at the window of the room where her father sexually abused her, annihilating her innocence with his sin. She picks up a stone and throws it, breaking the glass. She throws another and another until she falls on the ground, tears pouring from all the broken places of her soul. Forrest says gently, "Sometimes there just aren't enough stones."

There never will be, but talking out the wounds, the pain, the hurt you have experienced and carried with you for so long begins to heal your battered heart.

PRACTICE BOUNDARY-SETTING SKILLS

Because Barry had watched his mother's temper flare when he was a young boy, he had a huge disdain for anger even when it was appropriate. He didn't want to lose control. He equated anger with yelling and words you wish you could take back. I have had the privilege of watching him learn how to set good boundaries and own his anger when it is present.

We moved to a new home in the spring of 2001. Moving is always stressful, so we tried to be as organized as possible. Being an in-town move, we tried to do much of it ourselves and let the movers take just the heavier pieces. I have a lot of books. I packed them in boxes with "Sheila's office" in bold letters on the side and top of each one. Barry asked the movers to make sure all twenty of these heavy boxes went to my office. When the movers finished unpacking the van and left, Barry saw they had placed every one of the book boxes in the garage.

I popped my head into the garage to see what he was doing, and he said to me, "I need a little time to myself here!" I could tell he was furious. We talked about it later. He told me that it felt so good to be angry about something and be able to deal with it himself rather than stuffing it down or exploding like a Molotov cocktail.

DON'T GIVE UP YOUR BOUNDARIES
EITHER BY FIGHTING OR BEING PASSIVE

I've learned the value of time and space. As I learn to deal with anger issues, I know that when I have an overwhelming need to do or say something *right now*, it's probably better not to. Time and space allow me to sort out what's rumbling around in my head and heart, what's appropriate to the present situation, and what is old baggage.

WHEN YOU ARE READY, RESPOND

Much of each year I spend weekends on the road, traveling all over the country with Women of Faith. Saturday evenings after the conference wraps up are sacred turf for Barry and me. That's when we spend time with Christian. We take him out to dinner or do something fun that he would enjoy, either just the three of us or with the other speakers, our family away from home.

One weekend a woman I knew at a conference wanted to spend Saturday evening with me. When I explained to her how our family always spends that evening, she became very angry, accusing me of pretending to care about people but not being there when the rubber hits the road. The old me would have acted out of guilt and gone with her and left a very disappointed little boy at the hotel. Instead I told her that I was sorry she was upset. I gave her an address to write to me and reminded her that I had been available several times during the conference and this was Christian's time. She left, still angry. I prayed for her, but I let my no stand without feeling guilty that I am unable to meet the needs of everyone who crosses my path.

REGROUP

Talking incidents like this through with those we trust is very beneficial. It's hard not to second-guess ourselves when we're practicing new behaviors. I talked through the previous situation with a close friend and found her feedback very helpful. Sometimes we don't know what normal looks like or sounds like when we're practicing dealing with a volatile emotion like anger.

KEEP PRACTICING

It's wonderful to be free! Christ paid the ultimate price so that you and I could live with liberty and joy. Don't be controlled by angry people or allow anger to control you.

Calvary is the only place where perfect love embraced absolute hate. It is the place to take our refuse. It is the place to take our wailings and railings against this present reality.

In *Living Fearlessly* I wrote about a family who buried one of their sons four days before his twelfth birthday. I sit writing now on the one-year anniversary of Taylor's death. I have the privilege of being part of a prayer team that surrounds the remaining family members. We want to provide a safe place for them to talk about what is real, what is tearing them up, what they are afraid of. Taylor's father, Brian, is a gifted writer. The pain of watching cancer torment and ultimately kill your child is indescribable, as is the agony of praying passionately for physical healing and hearing no. One of the reasons I believe Brian is still "this side of the ledger" is his ability to pray out and write out his rawest emotions.

There are no spiritual Brownie points for pretending to be fine when we're not fine. There is enough dishonesty in prayer without editing what is consuming us. It's a strange phenomenon that we would try to hide what is true from God, the One who is more aware of all that is true than we will ever be. When we pray, we should pray out of who we really are rather than who we think God wants us to be.

Facing what is true is a step toward changing what we can. I talked to a woman who was a year into marriage number three and already in trouble. "He's just like all the rest," she said of her current husband. "He's mean and violent. I don't know why I married him." We talked for a while, and it became clear that she had never dealt with the violence she had experienced as a child. It was too scary for her to face that pain, and yet she kept choosing it in different suits over and over again. Our lives will deal us more of the same until we are willing to deal with what is true about our lives.

I had the experience once of singing at the Brooklyn Tabernacle Church in Brooklyn, New York. This amazing church reaches out to prostitutes, battered wives, drug addicts, crack babies, the broken, the bruised, and the disenfranchised. After the service I was awed by the number of people who stayed at the altar for a long, long time, weeping out loud, beating their fists on the floor, wailing the primal sound of a baby whose cry has been ignored.

The pastor, Jim Cymbala, saw the confusion in my eyes. "If you knew what some of these people go back to, you would understand why they stay here so long. They have a lot of stuff to get rid of." I've never forgotten that evening. It was one of the most honest things I have ever seen. It has helped me with Christian.

LITTLE CLENCHED FISTS

A few weeks after Christian's papa, William, died, I saw a change begin to take place in my son. He was angry. I was in the kitchen one day making soup when I saw him push our cat, Lily, roughly off her regular chair. He had never done that before. I disciplined him and told him what the consequences would be if he ever did it again. But there was something in his eyes that signaled more was going on inside him than was immediately apparent.

The next day I caught him kicking the door of his bedroom over and over again. We went for a walk.

"What's going on, sweet boy?" I asked him.

"I don't know," he said. "I don't feel good."

"Do you have a sore tummy?" I asked.

"No, Mommy. I hurt inside."

We sat down on the grass. "Are you angry, Christian?" I asked.

"Yes," he said, big tears pouring down his cheeks. "Why did God take my papa?"

"Papa was old, darling. He's gone to live with Nana and Jesus."

I saw his little fists clench. "I understand that you're angry, darling," I said. "And that's okay. But you need to find a way to be angry and not hurt yourself or Lily or anyone else."

I had an idea and bundled him into the car. We drove to a local sport store. I found the section with punching bags and asked the salesman if they had any for children. We found them, and I asked Christian to choose one. He picked an orange and black one with gloves to match. When we got home, I set it up in his playroom.

"This is a good place to take your anger, babe," I said. "When you feel mad, just come here and take it out on the punching bag."

He did, and sometimes so do I! I wonder how many children are rough at school or choose a violent path in life because they have never found a way to express their legitimate anger at the inhumanity of life or the injustice of the situation they find themselves in.

Anger in children is healthy and normal. A child who feels no freedom to toss his carrots across the room has learned too early that his world is not safe. The challenge for us parents is to teach our children responsible ways of expressing the God-given emotion of anger.

Sometime ago I became aware of a terrible situation. A family who had only recently become Christians were facing the news that the mother and two of the children, who were under six, all had cancer. I couldn't imagine how difficult that would be. They took trips to get their chemotherapy together. What a dark version of a family outing. Then the mommy died. My heart ached for the husband and for the surviving children who had to face the rest of their lives with no mom. A large group of us are on an e-mail list with the dad so that we know how to pray and what we can do to help practically. One of the last e-mails from the dad described the anger one of the children was carrying. "Any words of advice?" he asked.

I wrote back, promising my prayers and suggesting a trip to the sports store. Little clenched fists need a place to go.

I'm aware that some will be critical of my encouraging my son to vent his anger in this way. Is this what Jesus would do? Loving our enemies comes after recognizing what they are: enemies. I refer not just to people but to death, hate, violence, prejudice, fear; all the evil that surrounds us needs to be faced as the enemy. Only then can we begin to respond with a love as big as God's.

The fourth-century monks considered anger to be the most dangerous of all passions. They saw it as far more destructive than human greed or lust. Evagrius wrote that the remedy for all anger is prayer. He defined prayer as "the seed of gentleness and the absence of anger," and yet his community also defined it as "warfare to the last breath." In her book *Amazing Grace*, Kathleen Norris writes that when we quiet our hearts and minds to pray, old resentments often rise to the surface. That is the perfect time and place for them to emerge, she says, so they can be dealt with in the presence of God.

PLANTING SEEDS OF GENTLENESS

How do we teach our children to handle anger? Some kids are by nature aggressive, sensitive to comments from others, or simply seem to have a shorter fuse than most. How do we, by God's grace and under the shelter of his perfect love, plant seeds of gentleness in the hearts of our children?

First of all we as parents need to have our anger brought under the control of the Holy Spirit, or our words to our children will have no power. As Ralph Waldo Emerson said, "What you do speaks so loudly that I cannot hear what you say." Part of my own game plan for bringing my anger under control comes from 1 Peter 3:3-4: "Your beauty should not come from outward adornment, such as braided hair and the wearing of gold jewelry and fine clothes. Instead, it should be that of your inner self, the unfading beauty of a gentle and quiet spirit, which is of great worth in God's sight." Now if you asked my friends to pick a verse for me to meditate on regularly, I'm not sure they would immediately hit on this one! I love nice clothes. I have a shoe collection to rival Imelda Marcos's, although I get most of mine on sale. But I recognize that there is nothing more unattractive or defacing than a woman consumed by anger. So I copied out the verses in 1 Peter and stuck them on my mirror, my refrigerator, my car dash. Every day I was confronted by the truth of what is of great worth in God's sight. I prayed every single day for over a year that God would create a gentle spirit in me. It has made a huge difference in my life. I can't think of the last time when my anger was out of control. I still get angry, but it doesn't consume me.

Young children sometimes have a wrong or inaccurate picture of events. I see that in Christian. If someone accidentally bumps into him, he will get mad and say he never wants to see that person again. If he drops a book on his foot, he gets mad at the book, and I've seen him throw it across the room. Obviously this is not acceptable behavior, and Barry and I have worked to help him get an accurate picture of what actually took place. When he is mad, he can also do the "Aaoooga dance"! This is a family favorite. He goes outside and dances round and round and yells at the top of his voice, and then when he has calmed down, he comes in, and we talk about it.

But what about older children and teens where the anger can be destructive to their own lives and the lives of those around them? With the recent rash of explosive behavior that has turned school playgrounds into battlefields, it's clear that we have young people who have access to weapons and don't know how to handle anger.

In *The Parent Survival Guide,* Dr. Todd Cartmell suggests several things to help our children control their anger, beginning with God's Word in an age-appropriate translation. Children need to know what God says about anger:

> "In your anger do not sin": Do not let the sun go down
> while you are still angry, and do not give the devil a foothold.
> (Ephesians 4:26-27)

My dear brothers, take note of this: Everyone should be quick
to listen, slow to speak and slow to become angry, for man's
anger does not bring about the righteous life that God
desires. (James 1:19-20)

Dr. Cartmell suggests discussing this with our children when they
are in a good frame of mind and listening to them carefully. We can ask
questions like, "What are some of the things that make you angry?"
"Why does that make you angry?" "Why do you think God says we
should be slow to become angry?" "What do you think might be a better way of dealing with your anger?"

We can also help our children develop strategies to cope with life in
an unfair and unpredictable world. We can suggest productive rather
than destructive methods of handling themselves in stressful situations
that make them angry:

"You can walk away."

"You can say, 'No!'"

"You can count to ten before responding."

"You can memorize a scripture on anger and use it to direct your
emotions back to God."

Whether our children are four or fourteen, the greatest gift we can
give them is to teach them to pray, to trust God, to believe in his amazing and boundless love. What a privilege to teach children that they can
take their anger to God, pour the depth of their feelings on him, and
allow him to comfort and calm them. Children respond to honesty
from adults. We can share our struggles with them and tell them how
God is helping us to live in a way that is right and honorable. It is good
for anyone of any age to know, "I am not alone."

I discovered recently that I need bifocals. I was horrified. I am now
my mother, which must make her my grandmother! Christian saw my
glasses sitting on the table and asked me what they were.

"These are Mommy's new reading glasses," I said.

"Oh, cool. Can I try them on?" he asked.

"Sure. But things will look a bit funny."

He put them on and picked up a book. "You should take them back, Mom. They don't work. I still can't read!"

Praying out our anger, letting God purge us of the poison of resentment, and planting seeds of gentleness in the soil of our hearts and our children's is like learning to read. It's a process. It takes time and commitment. We cannot do it alone. Thank God, we are not asked to.

Suffering

I heard the voice of Jesus say,
"Come unto me and rest;
Lay down, thou weary one, lay down
Thy head upon my breast."
I came to Jesus as I was,
Weary, and worn, and sad;
I found in Him a resting place,
And He has made me glad.

—Horatius Bonar, "I Heard the Voice of Jesus Say"

7

SUFFERING

LOVE IN TEARS

My God, my God, why have you forsaken me?
Why are you so far from saving me,
so far from the words of my groaning?
O my God, I cry out by day, but you do not answer,
by night, and am not silent.

PSALM 22:1-2

It is worth noting that suffering only becomes a problem
when we believe in the existence of God.

DAVID WATSON

"All right, Papa. This time you be the Grinch who stole Christmas, and I'll be your dog, Max."

William dutifully mustered up his best Grinch face, and Christian got down on his hands and knees with a tree branch on his head like all good make-believe reindeer. "I'm going to steal Christmas," William said to me, trying to look threatening. My part was to represent all the people in Whoville on Christmas Eve. It was a big role.

"And we're not kidding!" Christian added with what was supposed to be a threatening sneer.

"Oh, please don't steal Christmas, Mr. Grinch," I begged tearfully. "Why don't you stay and have some roast beast?"

"No way, lady," William said.

"No way!" his dog added. "The roast beast is coming with us, and your Christmas tree and your cookies. Ha, ha, ha, ha!" His Machiavellian laugh filled the kitchen.

As Christmas of 2000 approached, it had become our after-supper ritual to play out the characters in the Dr. Seuss book *The Grinch Who Stole Christmas*. We alternated between that and the Nativity scene. Barry had the Nativity scene down pat. He was able to play all the major characters with a towel as his only prop. It was a real tearjerker. Tonight, however, he was in Florida on business, so the grinch had the floor. William, at eighty-two, was such a good sport. He had lived with us for almost two years, and we all loved the arrangement. He traveled with us everywhere we went, never complaining, although I knew at times he must have been exhausted. And he always had a smile and a wink for his only grandchild.

"All right, all dogs who want cookies and milk need to be in their baths in two minutes," I announced. Christian scampered off to the bathroom.

"I'll have my bath too, princess," William said. "Then I'll come down and kiss my boy good night."

Christian was bathed, tummy full of cookies and milk, yet William had not come down from his bath. I went upstairs to his bathroom and knocked on the door.

"Papa, are you all right?"

There was no answer. I knocked again. "William?"

I opened the bathroom door. William was lying on the floor, naked, his head in a pool of blood. I rushed over to him, grabbed a towel to put over him, and took his hand.

"Papa, what happened?"

"I don't know," he said. "I think I slipped."

I checked his head to see if the wound needed medical attention. It didn't seem too bad. I put a towel under his neck.

"I want to sit up," he said. I lifted him to a sitting position. "Oh no, that hurts. Lay me down," he said. I laid him back down, but he could not get comfortable.

I didn't know what to do. I was alone in the house with a three-year-old boy, Barry was in Florida, and William's lips were very blue. I called 911.

"Is he conscious, ma'am?" the emergency operator asked.

"Yes, he is, but he's not really making sense. Will you hurry please?"

I called Barry on his cell phone. He was watching a movie—a comedy. Before I could say anything, he said, "I need to take you to see this movie, babe. It's so funny."

"Barry, it's your dad."

"What? What's wrong?"

"I don't know, but I've called 911."

"Is he dying?"

"I don't know."

I heard Christian coming up the stairs singing a silly little song. I put my hand over the phone and called down to him.

"Christian, stay downstairs. I'll be there in a moment!"

"No, Mom. I'm coming up."

"Barry, I'll call you as soon as I know anything."

I wiped up the blood on the floor just as Christian reached the doorway. He stood still for a moment.

"What's wrong with Papa?" he asked.

"Papa doesn't feel very good," I said. "But we're going to get some help for him."

"Can I help, Mom?" he asked.

"Absolutely! Will you get a washcloth and put some cold water on it?" He did. "Now wring it out and put it on Papa's forehead."

We sat that way for ten minutes. Ten minutes was all we had left with William.

"Mom, look at the ceiling," Christian said.

I looked up and saw that the leak in William's bathroom had formed a large hole, and water was pouring through the plaster. One more ceiling made of paper in our money pit of a house. It seemed so trivial now. I held William's hand, and Christian sang to him,

You're so sweet
You've got sugar dripping off your feet.

As I heard sirens approaching, I realized that the front door was locked. I didn't want to leave Christian and William alone. I didn't want to leave William alone.

"Sweet pea, I have to open the front door. I'll be right back."

I tore down the stairs and opened the door. There were three emergency vehicles in the driveway.

"Where is he?" someone asked.

"Upstairs. First door on the left." I followed them up, taking two steps at a time.

"Christian, the men are here to help Papa. You come out here with me."

He sat on the floor in the corridor, thumb in mouth, his most available comfort. I watched as they got out the defibrillator; I realized they were losing my father-in-law.

"Christian. Will you do something for me?"

"Yes, Mommy."

"Will you get your backpack and put some things in it for Papa to take to the hospital?"

"Yes, Mom."

He scurried off to his room. I watched as the paramedics battled to save William. They brought him back once and lost him again. They brought him back a second time.

"Ma'am, we need to get him to the hospital. You can follow us there."

They lifted William onto a stretcher. I grabbed shoes and a coat for Christian to cover his pajamas. I found his portable DVD movie player and *101 Dalmatians,* and I ransacked the kitchen drawers looking for headphones.

"Let's get in the car, darling," I said. I got Christian buckled into his car seat. We waited. No one was moving. I got out of the car to see what was wrong. One of the medics came over to me.

"Wait for about ten minutes before you follow us," he said.

I didn't put two and two together. It was too surreal. I know now that William was already dead and they wanted time to lay his body out before I got there. But I didn't think that then. I thought they were working on him, making sure he was all right to transport. I suddenly thought about Barry again. I called him.

"We're on our way to the hospital," I said.

"I can't believe this," he said numbly.

"I know. I'm so sorry."

Christian and I drove in silence. My heart was pounding in my chest. "God, please don't let him die. We need him. We all need him." I parked in the emergency room parking lot, and Christian and I went into the ER.

"I'm here about William Pfaehler," I said to the girl behind the desk.

"Oh, yes," she said. "Just a moment." She made a call as I held Christian close to my heart.

"Please come this way."

I looked up to see a nurse in front of me. I followed her to a small, dimly lit room. "Is he all right?" I asked.

"Just wait here, ma'am. The doctor will be right in," she said.

I sat Christian in the corner and put his movie on. He plugged in his headphones and pulled them over his ears. I sat beside him. I looked up as the doctor came in. He saw Christian and stayed in the doorway. I went over.

"I'm sorry," he said. "We did everything we could."

I stared at him in disbelief. William had always been so healthy. We had been playing a game just a couple of hours before.

"Can I see him?" I asked.

"Yes."

A young, sweet nurse came and sat beside Christian. He ignored her and stared hard at the movie screen.

"He's in there," the doctor said. "Do you want to be alone?"

"Yes, please."

William was lying on a bed in a small room with a sheet over him, just his head exposed, so still, as if he had fallen asleep. I touched his face. He was still warm. I reached under the cover for his hand and squeezed it. He was gone. I laid my head on his chest and wept. "I will miss you, Papa."

"Blessed are those who mourn, for they will be comforted" (Matthew 5:4).

"Come on, darling. Let's go home," I said to Christian as I went back into the room where they take you when they have something bad to tell you.

"Is Papa coming with us?"

"No, darling. Papa's staying here tonight."

After driving in silence for ten minutes, my son said, "I will miss him, Mama."

I hadn't told him William was dead. He just knew.

Christian was asleep by the time we got home. I lifted him out of his car seat and put him in our bed. His backpack was still on his arm. I took it from him and pulled the covers up to his chin. I looked in his bag to see what he thought Papa might need at the hospital:

1 sucker
2 books
1 yo-yo
1 bear

A three-year-old's first-aid kit.

As I think back on that night now, my eyes fill with tears again. I cry because I miss William. I cry because Barry misses his father more than he realized he would. Even at thirty-seven you still feel like an orphan when your last parent dies. Mostly I cry for Christian. I would spare him this grief so early in life. I wanted his world to be full of only good things for as long as possible. I watch as he juggles between tears and pain, anger and helplessness.

For a while after his dad got home, Christian stayed a little distant from Barry, as if to say, "You weren't there. You don't understand." Often he questions himself and he questions me. "Did I do the right thing, Mommy? Did you do the right thing?" Then he questions God. "How big is God, Mom?"

"Bigger than anyone," I say.

"Does he have a family?"

"Yes, darling. He has a huge family."

"Then why did he take my Papa?"

Six months pass. We all try to adjust. Then one day, out of the blue, Christian announces, "I don't like God."

"Why don't you like God?" I ask.

"He took my papa. That was mean."

"WHY, GOD?"

"Why then did you bring me out of the womb? I wish I had died before any eye saw me" (Job 10:18).

What do you say to a child who doesn't understand suffering? What do I tell myself, for I don't understand either? How do we answer the "Why, God?" questions that pepper human history, machine-gunning our landscape? The only thing I'm convinced of is that it's critical to let the questions surface, as many as they may be, as raw as they may be. If we don't, then the fear and helplessness and resentment that pollute the soul will fester beneath the surface and slowly destroy our lives. But beyond being truthful about our pain, what are we to do? When all the pounding on the punching bag is through, when the yelling, screaming, or weeping begins to subside, what are we left with? How are we changed, and is it a good thing? Did God "make it happen" or "allow it to happen"—and is one any better than the other?

"Come to me, all you who are weary and burdened, and I will give you rest," Jesus promised (Matthew 11:28). When I am battered and bruised, sick at heart or sick in mind, he asks me to bring him my burden. And yet the burden I carry he could have taken away but didn't. At a deep secret place within me I wonder, *Are you jealous of anyone we love, God? If we loved everyone else less, would you let us keep them?* I know God isn't like that, but sometimes it seems that way.

In Psalm 46:10 the Lord says to us, "Be still and know that I am God." The life of faith is lived in commitment to God's sovereignty, to his being God, to our knowing that and what it means. I know that God is not a cosmic bully who loves to wield his sword because it's bigger than ours. I know that God aches with us in our pain. The divine mystery is that he loves us passionately, he is powerful enough to stop pain and suffering, and yet he doesn't do it. *WHY?*

Of course I don't know the answer to the trillion-dollar question any more than any other human being down through the centuries. But I do believe in the *P* word. I don't always like it, but I believe in it: process. I see it at work all around me.

Christian and I like to go to the ceramic store to paint. We choose a piece, choose our paint colors, and create! Last time I chose a mug. He chose a fish.

"I'm done, Mom," he said.

I looked at his fish. It had two green eyes, a partially painted tail, and that was it. "You are not done," I said.

"Yes, I am!" he replied happily as if he were passing on good news that would be a huge relief to me.

"You're not done, but I'll help you." I grabbed a brush, and we began to fill in the blanks on Flipper's frame. When we were done, we took it up to be fired.

"What a fine job you've done," the owner said as she took Christian's fish from him.

"Yes, and I did it all myself," he lied.

"That was a lie," I said as the woman turned her attention to another customer.

"You can be so negative, Mom," he replied. We had a little talk.

After he had suitably repented, we went for ice cream. When we were finished, he wanted to collect his fish.

"It's not ready yet," I told him.

"How long will it take?"

"Two weeks."

"Two weeks! That's too long. I want it now!"

I understand that. We all do. Perhaps even now you find yourself in a situation that is taking too long. You want it to be over. You want it to be over *now.* You feel out of control and helpless. So what is this process that is lauded by all who have gone through the fire and come out like shining gold?

In *Ruthless Trust,* Brennan Manning tells the story of a water bearer in India that beautifully illustrates the gift of process. The water bearer had two pots that hung on opposite ends of a pole that he carried on the back of his neck. One pot had a crack, while the other was perfect. Every day the perfect pot delivered a full measure of water when they arrived back at his master's house, the cracked pot only half a measure.

After some time the cracked pot told the water bearer that he was ashamed of his flaw. The water bearer told him to look at the flowers the next time they made the trip to haul water. The pot saw the flowers and was unimpressed. "Didn't you notice," the water bearer said, "that there are only flowers on one side of the trail? I knew your flaw and used it. I only planted seeds on your side of the road."

Manning urges us away from oversentimentalizing the story with a "We're all cracked pots" conclusion. Rather he urges us to see that so often we miss the point of our lives. We don't see God's grand purpose. Life is a beautiful, glorious gift, and God in his sovereignty is using you right now, where you are, in ways you can't even imagine. We want God to follow our game plan because it makes sense to us. He doesn't do that.

I used to believe it was my responsibility to make sure that Christian made all the right choices, understood the ways of God, and showed up for heaven with the right number of Brownie points. How ridiculous. God does not need me to be my son's public relations agent. As much as I love Christian, God loves him far more. My son is a flawed, sinful human being who will make mistakes and wrong choices; he will bleed and weep, and in all of it, God will be there.

Perhaps you read this and think, "Tell me that when your son is sixteen or twenty-six." Good point! What can I say? Only this: I believe in the goodness of God even though we are surrounded by pain. I believe that God can handle my son's questions. I believe that God can handle your child's rebellion and your heartache. I believe that God hears beyond our words to what is actually true and loves us, loves us, loves us.

We spend so much time trying to "market" God to one another. We try to explain his ways and make them popular and palatable. Where did we get the idea that this is our job? Our only job is to speak the truth about life and about God and *be there* with each other during the painful times. When Christian cries for the hundredth time and tells me that he misses Papa, I hold him and let him cry for as long as he needs to. My words won't patch up his wounds. There is actually a strange gift in his grief. I find myself thinking, *I wish you could see this, William. Did you know how much you were loved? You spent hour after hour reading stories, singing silly little songs, putting jigsaw puzzles together, and rocking this boy to sleep. Do you see what you sewed into the fabric of his soul? This is a good thing. We all want to be missed this much.*

I think of my prayer that night as Christian and I drove in silence to the hospital. "God, please don't let him die. We need him. We all need him." God could have answered that prayer with a yes. I could have arrived at the hospital to be told that it was a close one but William pulled through. We would have gone home and celebrated Christmas with a little more passion, a little more gratitude perhaps. But another moment would have come sooner or later. We do not live forever. Would it have been easier for Christian at seven than at three to lose his papa? I don't think so.

"WHERE WERE YOU, GOD?"

In the midst of writing this chapter, I took a break, poured myself a cup of coffee, and went upstairs to check in with Pat, who runs my office from our house.

"Did you have a good weekend?" I asked.

"Great, thanks," she said. "What about you?"

"We had fun. We played soccer and baseball and caught butter-flies."

"The pastor's message at church on Sunday was a good one," she said. "It was about Jesus' showing up late for Lazarus."

Just then the phone rang, and she ended up deep in conversation with a woman who wanted her to quote all the lyrics from my last CD over the phone. I left her to it. I couldn't get that thought out of my mind though. Jesus showed up late. It's an interesting story recorded in John 11. It has hope tucked inside every line if we will look for it.

Jesus was a dear friend of Mary and Martha's, sisters who had shown him hospitality before. He had spent time at their house, and he loved them and their brother, Lazarus. Mary, in particular, knew she could count on Jesus. She had once spilled expensive perfume on his feet and wiped them with her hair. She had held nothing back from her alabaster box. Now she and her sister needed Jesus to help them. No one else would do. Their brother was sick, sick enough for them to ask Jesus to come back to town when there was a bounty on his head. The message they sent was, "The one you love is sick." The implication was clear. "Lord, we've seen you heal others. We've seen you heal total strangers. This is Lazarus we're talking about here. This is someone you love, someone you have a relationship with. He needs you. He needs you *now*." I'm sure they didn't have a single doubt that Jesus would drop everything he was doing and get there fast.

He didn't do that. Instead he told the messenger that Lazarus wouldn't die, then he stayed right where he was. His disciples were relieved. They didn't want to go back to an area where the Jewish leaders had tried to stone Christ. Guilty by association, they might be hit by some of the stones. But two days later Jesus said, "Let's go!" They tried to resist and reason with him. Jesus answered them with a strange statement: "Are there not twelve hours of daylight? A man who walks by day will not stumble, for he sees by this world's light. It is when he walks by night that he stumbles, for he has no light" (John 11:9-10).

It must have been so hard for the disciples to figure out what Jesus was talking about half the time. Today we have the benefit of the whole canon of Scripture, of time, commentaries, and Bible study notes. The people in Jesus' day had nothing but what was passed on from rabbis, who studied the Old Testament text. The disciples say to Jesus, "Don't go back there. They tried to kill you!" And what does Jesus say? He answers with a breakdown of the structure of a day! But it's a great analogy if you think about it. What Jesus is saying is that God's timing is perfect. If we listen to God and trust him, we will walk in light. If we try to work it all out ourselves, we will stumble and fall in the darkness. Jesus did nothing by himself. His whole purpose was to do the will of the Father. This is our purpose too.

Jesus then tells the disciples that Lazarus is asleep and he will go now and wake him. They don't understand. It makes no sense. If Lazarus is just sleeping, surely someone else who is less likely to be stoned can cover the waking-up-Lazarus part. Jesus has to spell it out for them:

Lazarus is dead. He adds that he is glad for the disciples' sake that Lazarus has died. That seems like a cruel statement. Was Jesus really glad that his friend was dead and buried, that Lazarus's sisters were brokenhearted? No. Jesus simply wanted to teach them, teach us all, not to be afraid of death. He wanted to teach us that he is Life. He wanted to show us that all we are saying good-bye to down here is a temporary shell, and he can even breathe life back into a decaying corpse if he speaks the word.

It would have taken a day to walk the twenty miles back to Bethany. Lazarus has now been dead four days, and in the hot Palestinian climate, he has begun to rot. When Jesus arrives on the outskirts of town, Martha rushes to meet him. "If you'd been here, Lord, my brother wouldn't have died. But even now I know you could do something."

Jesus assures Martha, "I am the resurrection and the life. He who believes in me will live, even though he dies" (John 11:25). Jesus is perfectly calm. But when Mary hears that Jesus has arrived and rushes out to meet him, crushed with sorrow and accompanied by grieving mourners, Jesus is moved with profound emotion. We are told he burst into tears. I find that beautiful. I think he wept to see those he loved so broken. I think he wept for all of us. I think he wept for those of you who have stood by the bedside of a loved one and prayed for healing only to see life slip away. I think he wept for those who long to have a child but whose womb remains empty as a tomb. I think he wept for Barry, for Christian, for me. This life is a broken dream. It was never supposed to be this way, and it grieves our Lord.

Jesus lifts his voice and heart to God. He doesn't ask his Father to raise Lazarus; he thanks him that he has already done it. Raising Lazarus was crucial at this point in Jesus' earthly mission. It was as if he said, "I am here in flesh and blood. The dust of the road dirties my feet and stings my eyes too. If you cut me, I will bleed. When I see pain, I weep. But I am here because the Father sent me. Don't be afraid. Ask questions, cry, be human, be real. But know that when the dust settles, everything is going to be all right."

When Jesus called Lazarus to come out of the tomb, what he was saying could easily be interpreted, "Lazarus! This way out!" It's as if he were directing someone out of a maze. "Two steps left, one right, okay, straight ahead and you're home free."

> The dead man came out, his hands and feet wrapped with strips
> of linen, and a cloth around his face. Jesus said to them, "Take
> off the grave clothes and let him go." Therefore many of the Jews
> who had come to visit Mary, and had seen what Jesus did, put
> their faith in him. (John 11:44-45)

There is so much in this story if we will sit with it for a while with open ears. We miss so much because we're in a hurry to understand. It's not that grasping the implications of this story means we don't still ask questions, still weep and suffer. But we can be assured that our current heartache is not the end of the story. We are just weeping at the end of the first act.

Lazarus got an extension. That is the exception rather than the rule. If you have read any of my other books, you are aware that I have been greatly influenced by Gene Edwards's book *The Prisoner in the Third Cell*. John the Baptist did not receive the same unusual act of resurrection grace this side of heaven. When he put his head on the block, no one rushed in to rescue him. The underlying question of Edwards's book is a simple and profound one: "Will you love a God who does not live up to your expectations? Will you love God when there is no clear answer to the 'Why?'"

We cannot protect our children from things they don't understand. Death and suffering encourage all of us to ask the bigger questions: What is the purpose of life? Why are we here? We can't shelter our children from those basic questions or from the pain that comes with wrestling with them. But we can love them as they question and grapple. We can extend grace to them when they shake their fists at the inequity of life. We can forgive them when they know that in their pain they have crossed a line. We can let them speak what is true for them at that moment. Life is full of little losses and great losses, and there is no getting around that painful fact.

Christian has a Japanese fighting fish. His name is Red. He is actually Red Mark II, but Christian doesn't know that. Red Mark I was flushed and replaced. Red II is disgustingly healthy, and Christian decided he was lonely.

"You can't put another fish in with a fighting fish," I told him.

"But you could put one in a bowl beside him," he said.

So we ended up with two new goldfish, Marmalade and GI Joe. One morning at breakfast Christian said, "Look how quiet the fish are. They must be sleeping."

Even before I looked, I knew. They were both floaters! "Babe. I'm sorry, but they are dead," I told him as he tried to wake them up with a spoon.

He cried and cried. "Well, this stinks!" he said. "Now what?"

"We could bury them in a box, or we could flush them down the toilet," I said.

Much to my surprise he opted for the flushing funeral.

A few days later we were at the park. Christian was talking to a little girl from his Sunday school class. She was telling him all about her new dog.

"Do you know what I have?" he asked her.

"What?" she said.

"I have three cats, a dog, three fish, and a rabbit."

"Wow!" she said.

Wow! I thought.

As we were driving home, I said, "I heard you tell Mickey about your pets."

"Yes. I've got more than she does, Mom," he answered.

"Well, we don't actually have all of those pets living with us now," I reminded him gingerly.

"I know that," he said. "But just because they're gone doesn't mean they're not part of our family."

I learn a lot from my son.

There is something indecent about death. We are embarrassed by it. We don't know what to say, so sometimes we say ridiculous things. I remember spending time with a few of the mothers who lost children on that brutal day in Littleton, Colorado, when two boys took guns to school and changed the face of Columbine High School forever. One of the moms told me that at her son's funeral a woman asked her what she was going to do, decoratingwise, with her son's room now that he was gone!

Our children watch how we grieve with the same eagle eye that used to observe our joy and laughter. One of my most poignant memories of sharing grief with my son was on a three-hour plane flight. It had been some time since William's death. We were flying from Dallas to California. Christian was looking at a book, and I was working on my computer.

"Mama," he said.

"Yes, babe. What is it?"

"Look at that cloud. It looks like Papa's face."

I looked out the window. All I could see was a big puffy cloud that looked like a dragon to me. I looked back at Christian's face. Tears were gently falling down his silky cheeks. I took his hand. We sat there, side by side, tears streaming, holding hands in silence. We didn't need words. We understood. We sat with the loss, the void left by a darling man, but with the companionship of each other.

God longs to sit with you and hold your hand, no words smudging the silence. He wants you to know you are not alone.

HIS MYSTERIOUS WAYS

"Therefore we do not lose heart. Though outwardly we are wasting away, yet inwardly we are being renewed day by day" (2 Corinthians 4:16).

Lori Rickman has been a friend of mine for more than a decade. If you have read my book *Honestly,* you are familiar with some of her story. She was raised by adoptive parents in a very abusive situation. She left home and became a prostitute on the streets of Los Angeles. She used drugs and alcohol to anaesthetize the pain of not belonging anywhere but on the street. God pursued her, and she gave her life to him. Little did she know that her real problems were just beginning.

She has had surgery for two brain tumors. She has had a stroke. Now she has multiple sclerosis. She has no real income, so at the moment she is in a government-sponsored nursing home. Most of the people there are old and sick. She is in her thirties and confined to a wheelchair.

I have watched her struggle to survive so many things. I have sat with her in the intensive care unit of the welfare hospital in Los Angeles, and my stomach has turned at the unhygienic surroundings, the cockroaches on the floor, the smog coming through open windows. I have heard her question God so many times. I have echoed her questions. I have sat with her in a welfare psychiatric hospital, incensed as I see how they dope the patients to keep them quiet. She has faced so much, and now she sits in an institution where they only offer to bathe her twice a week and often they forget.

But something else is happening there. God is in the place. God is in his temple. God is working something remarkable in Lori. She e-mailed me this poem the other evening and told me I could share it with you.

LORD, IT'S THAT TIME AGAIN

Lord, it's that time again.
The light of the day has slipped away.
Everyone is sleeping but once again, I lie awake
Waiting for You to come be by my side.

This seems to be our time when I come to You.
Wearing no disguise,
Knowing I have no need for any walls.
No need to protect myself
From the One who knows and is All.
You meet me here.

I find You waiting for me.
I pour out from the depths of my soul.
You listen, as if You didn't already know.
But You know
For You are God.
Familiar with all that is me.
I find it hard to believe
That the Lord of All
Makes time for someone so small.

I find myself shedding tears.
My heart is on my sleeve.
So I come to You
Knowing You are all
I need.

As I pour it all out before You,
Like a sponge to water
You soak up every tear.
As You pull me close to You
And call me Your daughter,
You meet me here.

I find You waiting for me.
I pour out from the depths of my soul.

You listen, as if You didn't already know.
But You know
For You are God.
Familiar with all that is me.
I find it hard to believe
That the Lord of All
Makes time for someone so small.

You never cease to amaze me.
How You could love someone such as me.
Your grace overwhelms me.
Your mercy takes my breath away.
Your peace leaves me still.
Your gentleness has melted my hardness
Leaving space for only You to fill.

Yet Your faithfulness to me brings me to my knees,
As I know You are well aware of
The wandering of my heart.
Yet You've stayed by my side, never left.
As You whisper in my ear…
"Sleep well for I am here,
I will never leave you.
Just call out My name
And I'll be waiting
To meet with you once again."
You meet me here.

I find You waiting for me.
I pour out from the depths of my soul.
You listen, as if You didn't already know.
But You know

For You are God.
Familiar with all that is me.
I find it hard to believe
That the Lord of All
Makes time for someone so small.

Amen, Lori.
Amen, Mary and Martha.
Amen, William.
Amen, Red Mark I and Marmalade and GI Joe.
Do you see the quilt we have spread?
Love.
Grace.
Forgiveness.
A safe place to tell the truth.
A safe place to be afraid.
A safe place to be angry.
A safe place to ask why.

As parents, pain can seem almost unbearable, a load that will destroy our children. But sometimes the opposite is true. Again the mysterious ways of God break into my human understanding.

I met a woman in Dallas, Texas, whose story falls into that silent, holy place that only God could have created. She asked me to sign one of my children's books for her son. I have an ill-disguised affinity for sons, so I asked her to tell me about him.

"Well, he is ten years old and 100 percent handicapped. He can't speak, he is blind, but he is a trophy of God's grace," she said, a quiet smile on her face.

"What do you mean?" I asked, always probing to understand the ways of God in dark, unfamiliar alleys.

"When I hold him, he smiles. When I read to him from God's

Word, there is a quiet beauty that comes over him. His body stops twitching. He rests."

I asked her if I could have her address so that I could send future books to him. "That would be lovely," she said. "It will help him through the trial."

"The trial?" I said.

"We're in a bit of a bad place at the moment," she confided. "He was raped by a male nurse, and we are going to court."

I was silent, stunned.

"The nurse confessed to what he did, which will make the trial process smoother," she added.

"Are you telling me that a nurse, invited into your home to help your son, sexually assaulted a totally handicapped, helpless child?" I asked, anger rising in me as I tried to put myself in her place.

"He did."

"I would want to kill him with my own two hands," I said.

"I know. That's how I would have responded if I were listening to you tell me the same story. But you can't rule out God, Sheila. He shows up in ways you would never imagine. He's reminded me clearly that vengeance belongs to him, not to me. When you find yourself in the worst moments of your life, God's Word steps out of the page and becomes alive."

"Tell me what you mean!" I said, hungering for a richer taste of this mother's amazing faith.

"When this kind of pain and injustice invades your life, it's a rubber-meets-the-road moment," she explained. "Either God is real, or it's all a lie. Either God's Word is true, or we have no hiding place. I can't protect my son from every evil in this world. I thought I could, but I was wrong." She paused for a moment. "I choose to trust God, and that's what I pass on to my son. I don't understand all his ways, I don't like all his ways, but I trust him. I believe my son does too."

I'll never forget this woman or her son. In my search for answers to why, I find faith and trust in the souls of those whose hearts have been shredded by suffering. As Paul Tournier wrote, "The people who are the most alive are those who are the most torn."

Perhaps this is the greatest quilt to spread over our children. Perhaps it's the only one that won't let in the rain. We don't understand everything, but in the midst of our uncertainty and grief, we choose to embrace life and to lift our eyes and our hearts and our children to the Light of the world. His love is so big that it infiltrates even the darkest valleys.

Rebellion

O for a thousand tongues to sing
My great Redeemer's praise,
The glories of my God and King,
The triumphs of His grace.

He breaks the power of cancelled sin,
He sets the prisoner free;
His blood can make the foulest clean,
His blood availed for me.

—Charles Wesley, "O for a Thousand Tongues"

8

REBELLION

A Rejected Love

There is no one righteous, not even one; there is no one who understands,
no one who seeks God. All have turned away, they have together become worthless;
there is no one who does good, not even one.

ROMANS 3:10-12

The immediate result of this rebellion was a state of corruption
in which men were no longer able to distinguish between themselves and God,
and accordingly fell into idolatry, behind which, in all its forms,
lies in the last resort the idolization of the self.

C. K. BARRETT

The big day had arrived, and I was excited! Christian had been attending Toddler Time at our church for a year, and it was time for the Christmas presentation for the parents. The icing on the cake for me was that my mom had flown in from Scotland to spend Christmas with us, and she would be able to see what a brilliant, godly child her only American grandson is.

I had tried to get some details from Christian as to what the program entailed, but that familiar male well of minutiae was dry. Fortunately, Miss Dawn had sent a note home in his lunchbox on the previous day. She had indicated that the program would be short, as the children were not quite four, but they had learned a few Christmas carols, and each child had an instrument to play. I was very impressed. The children spent the morning rehearsing, and the parents were instructed to arrive after lunch for the big performance.

As one o'clock struck, we were all in our seats. Miss Dawn and Miss Mila, the teachers, welcomed us and announced that the first song would be "Jingle Bells."

"They start with the secular stuff and move on to the big finale: Joy to the world, Christ has come, I know I get presents, but I get it that this is about Jesus bit," I assured my mother.

Miss Dawn gave each child a tambourine. "How sweet!" I whispered to Mom, noticing that the instruments were decorated with Christmas ribbons. I bent over to get my camera from my purse.

"Stand in a straight line please, children," Miss Dawn said. "Christian! Stand in line please."

I heard that name, and my ears perked up. I stared at the front of the room like a deer caught in the headlights of a Mac truck. Christian had turned around and was standing with his back to the whole audience.

"Turn around, Christian," Miss Dawn repeated.

A few mothers gave me reassuring smiles. Just beneath the surface of each smile lay the silent but resounding message, "I'm so glad it's your child who's messing up and not mine!"

Miss Dawn decided to ignore my son, and the whole class gave a touching rendition of "Jingle Bells." But when they moved on to the spiritual stuff, Christian still wouldn't turn around.

I slipped out of my seat and went up to him. "What's wrong, darling? You love to sing," I said beseechingly.

"I hate singing, and I hate these dumb songs!"

I fanned myself. They were about to go into "Away in a Manger."

"Christian," I said with an edge to my voice that could have sliced four-year-old cheese, "you are being disobedient and disrespectful. Turn around immediately and join your class!"

I returned to my seat. My angelic son stood for the whole fifteen-minute performance with his back to the audience, his tambourine ribbons in Christmas green and red dragging the floor. I took one photo as a memento. There were eleven children dressed in colorful Christmas sweaters, faces aglow, and one child with his back to the lens so that all you could read was the back of his sweater: "I'm a Christmas angel." Fat chance!

We drove home in silence. Christian knew he'd messed up and that he was in trouble. As we pulled into the garage, I told him to go to his room and wait for me.

"I could sing my songs now for Grandma if you'd like," he offered.

"No thank you," I replied. "Just go upstairs and wait for me." He disappeared to his room.

"He's just a little boy," my mom said.

"He's just a little disobedient, disrespectful boy," I added. I went upstairs to Christian's room.

"Do you remember that we were supposed to be going to see the Christmas play tonight?" I asked him, alluding to a local production of "Raymond Briggs, the Snowman."

"Yes," he said. "I'll be very good and very respectful there."

"We're not going now," I said.

"Why not? You told me you'd take me!"

"Yes I did, but your behavior today was so naughty that you've lost that privilege," I told him. "I want you to sit here for fifteen minutes and think about why I'm upset with you, then we'll talk about it."

After I made Mom and me a cup of tea, I went back upstairs to talk to Christian. "Why do you think I was upset with your behavior today?" I asked him.

"Because I didn't sing the goofy songs?" he suggested.

"No, that's not it," I said.

"But I don't like those songs, Mom!" he said. "And my tambourine had girl stuff on it, and my sweater was goofy."

"I agree that the sweater was goofy, and I understand that you didn't want ribbons on your tambourine, but that is not the point," I said. "When you are in school, Miss Dawn is in charge. It is your responsibility to be respectful and obedient whether you like it or not."

I consider that one of my primary responsibilities as a parent: to teach Christian respect and obedience. It doesn't come naturally to him or to any of us. By nature we want to do what we want to do, when we want to do it. Paul wrote to Titus, "*Remind* the people to be subject to rulers and authorities, to be obedient, to be ready to do whatever is good, to slander no one, to be peaceable and considerate, and to show true humility toward all men" (Titus 3:1-2, emphasis added). To be subject in this context implies voluntary acceptance of a posture of submission. To be obedient is the visible demonstration of an attitude of humility.

Submission and humility are maligned words in our culture. They have been used to beat women into a corner emotionally and physically. They have been used as spiritual two-by-fours to shame our sisters and brothers in Christ. As an unfortunate result, we often forget Paul's admonition and stand in danger of missing our calling to be humble of heart and teachable in spirit.

I received a letter from a woman who was confused over this complex issue.

Dear Sheila,

My husband and I have been married for twelve years. We have five children. He wants to have more, but I'm exhausted as it is. We can't afford to have any more children. I don't know what to do. He says I have a spirit of rebellion. Do you know what that is? I looked it up in the back of my Bible, and it says that it's the spirit of witchcraft. Am I a witch? Please help me!

This woman's letter disturbed me so much that I decided to do a study on what the Bible really says about rebellion.

THE EVERLASTING "NO!"

When you hear the word *rebellion,* what springs to mind? Perhaps you think of a teenager brought up in a Christian home who decides to reject the moral and spiritual codes of his parents. You may think of runaways or see images of kids in bizarre clothes playing unintelligible music. Usually we associate the word with a departure from an acceptable standard of behavior. We often associate it with the young.

My understanding of Scripture on this issue leads me to conclude that rebellion is far more profound. I think it is an internal posture that would exalt the creature over the Creator. It is the ultimate rejection of divine love and unmerited favor. I think too that it comes in many religious disguises that are hard to recognize as rebellion, but rebellion they surely are. Rebellion, the kind of pride that would lead one to exalt himself above God, began with Lucifer.

> How you have fallen from heaven,
>> O morning star, son of the dawn!
> You have been cast down to the earth,
>> you who once laid low the nations!
> You said in your heart,
>> "I will ascend to heaven;
> I will raise my throne
>> above the stars of God;
> I will sit enthroned on the mount of assembly,
>> on the utmost heights of the sacred mountain.
> I will ascend above the tops of the clouds;
>> I will make myself like the Most High." (Isaiah 14:12-14)

"I will make myself like the Most High." That's the temptation, the sinful pride and ambition that lead to outright revolt. As we seek to love our children and tend their malleable hearts, it would be wise to take another look at the whole issue of rebellion, for it is far more insidious than simply refusing to eat one's carrots.

Personality type seems to be built into our very genes as we're formed in the womb. Some children accept everything they're told, while others question every little detail of life. This is not necessarily rebellion; it is largely the natural makeup of a highly inquisitive child. Obviously that kind of questioning mind still has to be brought under submission to self, to parents, to teachers, and to God in respect and obedience. But a strong-willed, curious child is often mislabeled as rebellious.

Our son questions everything.

"It's bedtime," I say.

"Why?" Christian asks, looking up from his pirate ship.

"Because tomorrow is a school day."

"But I'm in the middle of a battle!"

"You'll just have to finish the battle tomorrow," I say.

"Mom, battles don't work like that," he replies indignantly.

"This one does," I assure him.

"But it's still light outside," he adds.

"That's because summer is coming. But it's still your bedtime."

"Why does it stay lighter in summer? Why can't I wait until it's dark? Where did the moon go? How can I sleep if I'm not sleepy? I think I might have a fever. I feel a little nauseous. The cat's still awake. The fish has fainted!"

On and on and on and on. My challenge is to respect my child's mind, answer as many questions as I can, laugh a lot, and make it crystal clear that when I tell him something, it is not a suggestion; it is what we will be doing. Christian's strong will, sharp mind, and sinful nature make themselves known most days, as do mine, and one of my privileges as a parent is to corral his behavior, discipline him when necessary, and teach him about humility, respect, repentance, and forgiveness. As I have said, I am a strong advocate of grace but not at the cost of minimizing what our sin did to the Lamb of God. Grace can only be grace when the depth of our sin is understood.

When Moses came down from receiving the Ten Commandments on Mount Sinai and saw the debauchery and idolatry that God's people had thrown themselves into, he smashed the very words of God at their feet. But God did not give up on his rebellious children. He told Moses to cut out two new stones and return to the mountaintop. There God passed before Moses, showing himself and saying, "The LORD, the LORD, the compassionate and gracious God, slow to anger, abounding in love and faithfulness, maintaining love to thousands, and forgiving wickedness, rebellion and sin" (Exodus 34:6-7). But he added this: "Do not worship any other god, for the LORD, whose name is Jealous, is a jealous God" (Exodus 34:14).

We sin, we make mistakes, we willfully choose to do what we know is wrong, and our compassionate God provides a way for us to be washed clean. What God will not tolerate, however, is ongoing idolatry—an elevation of anything or anyone besides him to the top of the list in our lives. We belong to him, not to ourselves (1 Corinthians 6:19-20). Going after whatever we want whenever we want is not an option.

My sister, Frances, was in a production of Goethe's *Faust* when she was in college. I was horrified! Not only were there skimpy costumes on stage, but there was also a scene in hell. "Doesn't she know that we are good Baptists?!" I asked my mother. Out of loyalty to my big sister, I went to the opera with my mom, hoping that perhaps I could lead someone to Christ at the intermission.

Faust is a powerful tale of a man who sells his soul to the devil for the gift of eternal youth. It is a story of damnation and salvation. It is the more familiar of the operas on this theme, but Arrigo Boito's *Mefistofele,* though not as well known, depicts a scene in heaven where Lucifer presents himself before God, bringing his dissent into the holy place. "Mefistofele is the embodiment of the everlasting 'No!' addressed to the True, the Beautiful, and the Good," wrote Boito.

What a succinct and profound description of the spirit of rebellion. We were created to be obedient worshipers of a perfect Being, not little gods of our own making who embody the "no!" of our own puny wills. When we elevate ourselves as more powerful than God or put our will before his, we will pay a price.

> Or do you show contempt for the riches of his kindness, tolerance and patience, not realizing that God's kindness leads you toward repentance?
>
> But because of your stubbornness and your unrepentant heart, you are storing up wrath against yourself for the day of God's wrath, when his righteous judgment will be revealed. God "will give to each person according to what he has done." To those who by persistence in doing good seek glory, honor and immortality, he will give eternal life. But for those who are self-seeking and who reject the truth and follow evil, there will be wrath and anger. (Romans 2:4-8)

When Paul wrote his letter to the believers in Rome, he spoke right to the matters at hand among them, but the same issues continue to resonate in generation after generation. The consequences of the deliberate rebellion Paul speaks of in the first three chapters of Romans are powerfully portrayed in the Milos Foreman film *Amadeus*.

NO OTHER GODS

I remember the impact that movie had on me the very first time I saw it. It is the story of the great rivalry between the young genius composer Wolfgang Amadeus Mozart and the older Royal Court composer Antonio Salieri. The movie begins at the end of the story and then goes back in time to explain the angst-filled opening line: "Forgive me, Mozart!"

Those words spring from the tortured mind and soul of Salieri. He utters these words too late for Mozart to hear them. By this point in the story, Mozart is dead. Salieri, bitterly jealous of Mozart, had set out to systematically destroy him and, believing that he was solely responsible for accomplishing this, is overwhelmed with guilt. He survives Mozart by thirty-four years but lives in relative obscurity. "I was born a pair of ears, and nothing else," he reflects toward the end of his life. "It is only through hearing music that I know God exists. Only through writing music that I could worship."

In the young Mozart, Salieri meets someone who hears better than he, who writes music better than he. He is consumed by rebellious hatred. Why would God give Mozart the gift that Salieri has longed for all his life? In his bitter rage he conspires to destroy his rival, but even after Mozart is dead, Salieri realizes that he will never take his place; all he will ever be is the Patron Saint of Mediocrity.

Finding no balm in Gilead, no place to wash his bloodstained hands, he then attempts at the age of seventy-three to take his own life. Even that attempt is thwarted. Servants break down his bedroom door, and Salieri spends the remainder of his days, three more years, in an insane asylum.

The journey to that walled cage of mind and body began years before. As a young boy, years before he met Mozart, Salieri prayed to God, "Make me great.... Make me famous through the world. Make me immortal. Let everyone speak my name with love. In return I promise you...my chastity...my industry...and my deep humility." Salieri longed for the Divine to be placed in him. He longed to have that touch of heaven, that genius that would set him apart from other mortals.

Shortly after that prayer Salieri's pursuit of his dream of being the greatest composer the world had ever known took him to Vienna, where he eventually became the court composer for Emperor Franz Joseph II. Peter Shaffer, who wrote the original stage play of *Amadeus,* said this of Salieri: "He sought to snatch the Absolute." He wanted to "blaze like a comet across the firmament of Europe." But God says, "You shall have no other gods before me" (Exodus 20:3). Paul wrote about that in his letter to the Romans. "They exchanged the truth of God for a lie, and worshiped and served created things rather than the Creator—who is forever praised. Amen" (1:25).

When we think of rebellion in our children, we often see it as their rejection of our ideas and dreams. In Salieri, however, we see the truer face of the rebellion condemned in Scripture. It is a rebellion against God's plans, God's ways, and God's choices.

Your son is a soccer player. He is good. You do everything you can to give him opportunities to pursue his goals. Someone else gets picked over him. Someone else's son has that edge that sets him apart. What do you do? How do you handle that? How do you model the love of God in that context?

Your daughter is a singer. She tries out for a recording contract. Someone else in your church has a daughter who tries out at the same time. You know this girl. You know her morals are a little shaky at best, but when she opens her mouth to sing, she sounds like an angel. Why? Why would God put such a gift in an unclean vessel when your daughter has kept herself pure for God and his service?

We ignore the lessons of Mozart and Salieri at our peril. God is the one who decides where to place his gifts, and when we rebel against his choice, we rebel against him.

CARDBOARD BOXES

Robert Jewett's book *Saint Paul at the Movies* imagines a dialogue between the apostle Paul and the popular culture of Hollywood in the twentieth century. It's not such a far-fetched idea. We think of Paul on mission trips, writing letters from exile, but Paul had a day job. He was a tentmaker. He spent a large part of his life as a blue-collar worker. Paul lived as a theologian in the marketplace of his day, trying to bridge the gap between the cultures and religions around him.

Jewett asserts that many in modern-day culture are far more influenced by videos and movies than by formal education or religious training. That is certainly true of children. In 1993, when Jewett wrote his book, twenty million people a week went to see movies. Home video rentals were eighty million weekly. Think how high the numbers are now, several years later! Jewett's challenge to us is to hear and enter into the dialogue that is going on in our culture and counter it in the minds and hearts of our families with what is good and true.

USA Today reported in its 30 May 2000 edition that in one year the average American child spends nine hundred hours in school and one thousand hours watching television. Some movies depict the arrogant spirit of Lucifer, who tries to exalt himself above God. Others are powerful rewrites or dramatizations of some of Paul's letters. Such is *Amadeus*. It is a powerful teaching tool for older children and certainly for us as parents regarding what the spirit of rebellion really is: shaking our fist in the face of God, offended by his will, his choices, and his ways.

Mozart is the most obvious sinner in the movie. He is uncouth, immoral, a glutton and philanderer. It is easy to recognize him as such. But Mozart was also a genius. He wrote his first concerto when he was four. He wrote a whole opera by the time he was twelve. When Salieri reviewed some sheet music by Mozart, he was staggered to see that there were no corrections. Mozart heard everything in his head, perfectly, the first time. Salieri recognized in Mozart's genius the divine gift that he had coveted for himself. Mozart had what Salieri wanted. He had the gift Salieri believed God *owed* him. Didn't they have a deal? Why would God put such creative genius in an uncouth, filthy vessel? Mozart was an upstart. He was the "classic" sinner. His own father was disgusted with him, his bishop all but washed his hands of him, and the royal court thought him arrogant and improper.

In light of what Paul wrote to the Romans, however, Salieri appears guiltier of the more chronic sin. Seeing that God had chosen Mozart, an unclean vessel, over the pristine vase that he viewed himself to be, Salieri declared war on God. He completely missed the truth that all we are, even at our finest and most gifted moments, are earthen vessels to contain the treasure of God. We are never more than common receptacles to display the power of God.

If we could begin to grasp this powerful truth, I believe it would revolutionize our lives and spill over onto our families and friends. We live in a culture that elevates giftedness. We worship the thin, the beautiful, the geniuses of our day. We teach our children that if they want to "be someone," it's their performance that will guarantee they are appropriately recognized.

A Women of Faith conference was already booked into an arena for a weekend when the arena staff realized that they had double booked us with a dog show! Neither group could move the dates, so we coexisted. We were given the large, upstairs arena, and the dog show was given the smaller one downstairs. It worked fine, although the book tables were right beside the dog preparation area. Luci Swindoll and I had fun with that, moving signs around. Over our table we had "Please keep your grooming area clean!" "Wipe up your own messes," "No dogs in the bathroom."

I watched part of the dog show that night on the local news, and it struck me that I would not do well in a dog show. They are judged totally on performance and grooming. I could never keep my tail up that long! But don't we carry that mentality into our Christian lives and consciously or unconsciously pass it on to our children? So often our indignation at their bad behavior is simply a reflection of our own pride:

We're afraid their naughtiness or downright wickedness will reflect badly on us (like a certain mother I heard of whose son stood with his back to the crowd during a Christmas performance!).

When Paul told the church in Corinth that all he was in his best or his most sinful moments was an earthenware pot, that was a shock to their system of thinking and judging. His choice of the jar of clay metaphor could not have been more perfect. The pots in his day were common, imperfect, cheap, of no value in themselves. They absorbed the fragrance of what was kept in them. Corinth was a large, bustling city—a manufacturing hub and a major seaport. According to Paul Jewett, what the apostle said, in effect, was, "We are only cardboard boxes." The box is not the point! The box will never be the point. The box's only purpose is to be a container. The treasure inside is from God.

God deposited great treasure in the shabby box of Wolfgang Amadeus Mozart's life. Salieri missed that truth. He wanted to *be* the treasure, and when God put more in Mozart's box than Salieri perceived he had placed in his, he rebelled against God. "From now on we are enemies, you and I," Salieri declared. It's not that he lost faith in God. It's not that he no longer believed God existed. His was a far greater sin. He believed God existed, but he made the wrong choice anyway. His declaration of war on God is chilling. "I will block you, I swear it. I will hinder and harm your creature on earth. As far as I am able, I will ruin your incarnation."

He disguises himself in a mask that Mozart's father had worn at a masquerade ball, and even as he terrifies Mozart, he commissions him to write a requiem. Salieri's twisted plan is to claim the work as his own and use it at Mozart's funeral. He can think of no finer way to "hinder and harm," to thwart God's plan.

Rebellion corrupts not just our hearts but also our minds until we can no longer reason. We lose all sense of what is right and wrong. We stride and leap across healthy and proper boundaries, and our lives spin out of control. Salieri lived for music, and yet in his sickness of soul, he got up every morning determined to destroy it in Mozart. Rebellion not only destroys what we hate in others; it also destroys us. "Furthermore," warns Paul, "since they did not think it worthwhile to retain the knowledge of God, he gave them over to a depraved mind, to do what ought not to be done. They have become filled with every kind of wickedness, evil, greed and depravity" (Romans 1:28-29).

FILLED WITH LOVE AND TRUTH

There are so many important things to teach our children. There are shelves of books on all the rights and wrongs, the good and bad, the worthy and unworthy. But it is up to us to discern God's will in regard to our own lives and how we parent our children. We are responsible.

Let me give you a small example. I was looking for a good pediatric dentist for Christian. I made some inquiries and found a practice that I decided to check out. I made an appointment for us to meet the dentist and have her familiarize him with what goes on. I wanted it to be fun for him. I was terrified as a child by the huge man that towered over my mouth removing things that I was sure I'd need at a later date, and I wanted my son's experience to be different. The dental office seemed welcoming, so as Christian played with toys, Barry began to fill in the required forms.

"Look at this!" he said. I looked at the sheet he was holding. "Parents are not allowed into the room with their children. There will be no exceptions."

I marched up to the front desk! "This is Christian's first visit. I'm assuming I can at least come back with him to meet the dentist."

"Absolutely not, ma'am," the receptionist replied.

"You expect me to let my four-year-old son disappear through that door by himself to meet a total stranger?" I asked incredulously.

"If you want him treated here, yes," she replied with an "I can handle you, lady" look in her eyes.

"Well, I guess I don't then," I said. We left.

That may sound like an overreaction of an overprotective mother, but that is my job. It's my responsibility to protect my son when he is young. It's my job to watch what he's watching on television. It's my job to screen the videos he sees and the books he reads. There is a world out there that would love to teach my son to rebel, and I don't just mean standing with his back to an audience. The enemy of his soul would teach him to be a god in his own right, to elevate himself over all authority.

In a 1986 issue of *Theology Today*, Samuel Terrien wrote in his article "Amadeus Revisited," "Because the religious man feels deceived, his belief turns into blasphemy. Because the moral man feels cheated, his virtue turns into a trough of malevolence." What are we teaching our children to believe? If we raise our children to believe that God owes them a happy life, then they will be disillusioned. If we teach them that if they just have enough faith, their lives will be like a perfect three-act play, then they will become bitter. If we teach them that they are anything more than cardboard boxes, then we do them a disservice.

That's a fine line to walk. As parents we want to build our children up. I tell Christian every day that he is the most wonderful boy in the whole wide world. I want him to have an intact ego in the purest sense of that word. But at the same time it is my job to teach him that everything good in him is from God. That's why every night before he goes to sleep and before he says his prayers, we look back at the day and have our "What are we thankful for today?" time. He usually asks me to go first.

"Well, I'm thankful for the fun we had at the park. I'm thankful for the wind that made our kite fly so high. I'm thankful that God helped me write five pages of my new book today," I say.

"But *you* did that, Mom," he interrupts.

"Everything good I do comes from God, sweet pea."

"But I saw you in your office," he continues. "You were in there by yourself, except for when that cat jumped through the window."

"Just think of Mommy's life as a big toy box that God fills with good things," I say. "Everything that you or I pull out is only there because God put it there in the first place."

"Hmm." He mulls this over for a moment. Then it's his turn. "I'm grateful for my mommy. She is a fun toy box."

Mozart ended up buried in an unmarked grave. Salieri died in an insane asylum. Was one man better off than the other? In the end was one's sin greater than the other's?

Mozart wrote his forced requiem. As a young woman I sang the words of the beautiful piece "Kyrie Elieson" without understanding them. I was stunned to realize later that they are words of forgiveness and reconciliation. They are words of the great love of God poured out on all of us, for surely we are all at times Amadeus or Salieri.

Rebellion is part of the human package. Our sinful nature pulls at our calling to humble ourselves before God. Our innate pride tempts us to take credit for what is good in us and to place blame on the shoulders of someone else for what is sinful. I daily repent of the sin of elevating myself into the place that belongs to God and to God alone. It is ridiculous to think of a cardboard box vaulting itself over its contents, but it is all too easy to forget that is all I am.

When we moved recently, I contacted a company that provides moving supplies. The representative asked me if I wanted new or used boxes. "Are the used ones in good shape?" I asked.

"Oh they're fine. They're just used," she said.

"Are they as strong?" I wanted to know.

"Yes. They might have some tape on them. They might not be so perfect on the outside, but they're just as strong," she told me.

The box is not the point! Some of us might look more together on the outside, but even the most perfect box is just that: a box. I am brought to my knees by the knowledge that the love of God is so great, so big, so gracious, that he will fill up empty boxes like us with himself. And even when we get clogged up with our own importance, he will clean us out and fill us again with the divine treasure of his love and truth—with himself.

"But we have this treasure in jars of clay to show that this all-surpassing power is from God and not from us." Paul's words to the church in Corinth ring out a warning to us and to our children today. The Corinthians were very impressed with themselves and not very impressed with Paul. They considered themselves super apostles and Paul a bit of a loser. Paul appeared weak; he was shipwrecked, imprisoned, beaten, run out of town. That's the whole point of the passage and an enormous truth and challenge to us as we parent our children. What makes Paul such a shining example is that obedience was more important to him than a glossy résumé.

In our culture we despise weakness and exalt strength. I watch the competitive streak in my son. He wants to be the best, the coolest, the most handsome, the winner. The challenge before Barry and me is to help him aim high but remain humble, knowing that every good thing that is in his box is a gift from God. As you parent your own children, one of your most important jobs is to help them be good stewards of the gifts God has placed within them and at the same time rejoice at the gifts God has placed in the ones who sit beside them, even if those are the gifts they might be tempted to sell their souls for.

Antonio Salieri sought immortality. He was willing to pay any price to get it. At the end of his story and in his madness, he declared that now he had achieved his goal. "As his [Mozart's] name grows in immortality, so will mine—if not in fame, then in infamy. I'm going to be immortal after all. So, Lord, see now if man is mocked!"

If you are wise, your wisdom will reward you;
 if you are a mocker, you alone will suffer. (Proverbs 9:12)

"Forgive me, Mozart!"

Peace

When peace, like a river, attendeth my way,
When sorrows like sea billows roll;
Whatever my lot,
Thou hast taught me to say,
"It is well, it is well with my soul."

Though Satan should buffet, tho' trials should come,
Let this blest assurance control,
That Christ has regarded my helpless estate,
And hath shed his own blood for my soul.

And, Lord, haste the day when the faith shall be sight,
The clouds be roll'd back as a scroll,
The trump shall resound and the Lord shall descend,
"Even so," it is well with my soul.

—Horatio G. Spafford, "It Is Well with My Soul"

9

$=$ PEACE $=$

An Abiding Love

But the wisdom that comes from heaven is first of all pure; then peace-loving,
considerate, submissive, full of mercy and good fruit, impartial and sincere.
Peacemakers who sow in peace raise a harvest of righteousness.

JAMES 3:17-18

This is a sane, wholesome, practical working faith:
That it is a man's business to do the will of God;
second, that God himself takes on the care of that man;
and third, that therefore that man ought never to be afraid of anything.

GEORGE MACDONALD

I was sorting through some boxes one day when I came across a letter my mother sent to me. She knew it would make me smile. I read it again and again and laughed. It was from an Egyptian family who had lived next-door to her in Scotland for a couple of years. The husband was a student at our local agricultural college. His spoken English was pretty good, but his wife didn't speak any English at all, and my mother's Egyptian can be summed up in two words: *pharaoh* and *pyramid*. Despite the language barrier they had become friends of sorts.

When the husband finally graduated, the family went back to live in Egypt. A few months later Mom received an updated photo of the family along with this letter:

Dear Mrs. Walsh,

I hope this litter finds you welling. I hope you enjoyed too much
during your holiday in USA. We are back thanks for the God
and in good mode. Well here we are and there you are. Yes, this is
it. Hope to see you in Egypt.

Thank you for all your pile of friendship!

I laughed till tears rolled down my cheeks. I knew exactly what he
meant, but it didn't come out quite right. Like the time Mom and I
were in Paris and I told her that my French was so fluent I would be able
to order for both of us. She wanted chicken, and I wanted steak. I
thought that was what I had ordered, but we ended up with four salads
and enough lettuce to feed a field of rabbits until the Second Coming
of Christ. Or the time when I lived in Holland, working for Youth for
Christ. I stayed for a month with a family who spoke no English, and I
spoke no Dutch. When I was leaving, the wife said something to me
that sounded like "Hooden Fooden Booden." I smiled and said,
"Oh, yes. Thank you!" and ended up with a pile of her daughters' old
sweaters!

Language is a fascinating gift. I love words and dialects, but I am not
a letter writer. I sit staring at a blank sheet of paper, willing words to
appear before me. That probably sounds strange since writing is a big part
of my profession, but the truth is I hate to write letters! I don't even like
to send faxes or use the phone to talk to those who are dear to me. I like to
talk to my family and friends face to face. I like to look in their eyes.

The apostle Paul, however, had few options when it came to
communicating with those he loved. His passion was to disciple the
fledgling churches under his care, and the main vehicle for communicating was letter writing. Paul began all his letters with the same
wonderful greeting, peculiar to him, "Grace and peace to you." This took

the traditional Greek greeting, *chairein,* and elevated it to that glorious word, *charis:* God's unmerited favor. He combined this with *shalom,* the Hebrew word proclaiming a peace that comes from God alone.

What a greeting! *Charis.* Grace poured upon us for no other reason than he is God and he loves us with a love so big it broke his heart. *Shalom.* Peace in a world continuously erupting in turmoil, torn by chaos and dissension. Peace to families who stare at each other across the room and wonder who they have become.

What does *shalom* say to you? Is peace a reality in your life and in your home right now? I believe with all my heart that it can be, no matter what is true at the moment, because Christ can change anything—especially our own hearts. Peace is an internal reality. It is a gift from God that transcends our daily circumstances and is not dependent on everyone else in our life accepting the same gift.

Think of the disciples. They had just lived through the worst weekend of their lives. John had watched the whole thing. He had seen the nails driven deep into the wrists and ankles of Christ. He had held up Jesus' mother, Mary, as she watched her boy be torn apart. Surely he had heard that dark, primal cry, "My God, my God, why have you forsaken me?" How could he ever forget that sound? For in it was every question and tear and brokenhearted disappointment in the world. It was a cry that literally blocked out the sun.

And what about Peter? How would he ever know a day of peace again in his life? How would he ever close his eyes at night and not see Christ's eyes as he predicted that Peter would betray him? What tore at Peter's heart like a familiar fishhook was that Jesus hadn't looked angry, just sad and knowing.

When the whole bloody ordeal was over and Jesus had been laid in a tomb, there were questions, accusations, and doubts among his disciples. No peace. In fact, Jesus' best friends had hidden themselves behind locked doors, hiding in fear of the Jews who had put Jesus to death. And yet while they were cowering in fear, Jesus himself miraculously appeared among them and said, "Peace be with you!" (John 20:19).

Can you imagine that moment? First of all, their Lord was alive! Were they dreaming? Could it be true? Then what did that mean? Were they now to go out and slaughter their oppressors because they had a risen-from-the-dead Superhero? The glorious paradox is that even at that moment, when finally they saw that Jesus was indeed the Christ, the Messiah, all the rules changed and they became men of peace. Their first commission from the Lord was to spread his message of peace and reconciliation to the world. "Again Jesus said, 'Peace be with you! As the Father has sent me, I am sending you.' And with that he breathed on them and said, 'Receive the Holy Spirit. If you forgive anyone his sins, they are forgiven; if you do not forgive them, they are not forgiven'" (John 20:21-23). After Jesus blessed his friends and ascended to heaven, "Then they worshiped him and returned to Jerusalem with great joy. And they stayed continually at the temple, praising God" (Luke 24:52-53).

These were changed men! No longer captive to their fear, their anger, their sorrow and confusion, they threw open the locked doors and went out to live boldly for their risen Lord.

Even as I write this, tears stream down my face, and I want to get down on my face and worship. Only God can take sinful, stubborn men and women like you and me and transform us from the inside out. He doesn't just change our behavior; self-help tapes can do that. But Christ transforms us in such a way that there can be no doubt he is the One at work.

So look at your situation now. Look at your heart as I look at mine. Left to my own devices I would be a controlling, angry, fearful woman who would leave claw marks on the souls of those I love in a desperate attempt to get what I think I'm looking for. But, praise be to God, I am not left to my own devices, and neither are you. The whole point that we miss a hundred times a day is that we were never expected to live to impress God; he alone impresses himself upon the world *through* us. We are not performing seals; we are cardboard boxes.

THE PARADOX OF PEACE AND PAIN

What image comes to mind when you think of a peaceful place? A group of artists was asked to paint something that would epitomize the concept of peace. Many drew the traditional landscapes of water, sunset, and quiet beaches that we tend to associate with peace as if it were a place. One artist drew a very different picture, however, that I believe gives a much clearer picture of what peace means to a Christian. His canvas was wild, stormy, and threatening; but if you looked carefully, you could see a tiny bird tucked inside a cave in the side of the mountain. The storm was all around, but the bird was held in a protected place. "For in the day of trouble he will keep me safe in his dwelling; he will hide me in the shelter of his tabernacle and set me high upon a rock" (Psalm 27:5).

One of my favorite photos shows Barry carrying Christian on his shoulders. Barry's arms are locked around Christian's feet, anchoring him in place. That is how our Father carries us. The storm may roar around us, but we are held firmly by our Father, safe above the squall.

One of the most interesting women I have ever interviewed is Dr. Diane Komp, Professor of Pediatrics Emeritus at Yale University School of Medicine. She is a warm, compassionate woman who came to love God through watching children die. I don't say that lightly. It sounds impossible, obscene, until you listen to her.

As an expert on treating cancer in children, Dr. Komp has watched children suffer, held mothers as they weep, and stood in silent empathy beside fathers as they kick wastebaskets across her office enraged by their inability to tame this monster who torments their child. I would think that watching that kind of pain would make you doubt the very existence of God. I asked her about that when I interviewed her several years ago. "It is a humbling thing to watch how Jesus meets children when they die," she said. "I could not doubt his existence."

Suffering gets us right to the heart of the matter: Either God exists or he does not. Either he loves us or he does not. Suffering kicks us out of the procrastination party line and calls for a response. It calls for a decision, a yes! or a no! Komp's book *Why Me?* is one of the best things I have ever read on the paradox of peace and pain. She uses the life of Job to lace together the stories of the "Jobs" she meets every day.

I wondered, *If you watch cancer ravish children every day, does it become a demon that haunts your sleep?* Dr. Komp relates a conversation about that in her book. She is on her way to the house of a teenager who is dying of cancer. She takes with her a seminary student. On the way the student asks, "Are you afraid of cancer?"

"No, not really," she answers. "I don't like cancer at all, but I've learned so much from the children I care for that I think the fear has gone out of me."

That's amazing and comforting to me. There are Jobs all around us who have been through unspeakable tragedy and yet rise from the ash heap with a brilliance they are unaware of and a peace that nothing can shake. Peace is possible, no matter what you are facing right now, because God's love is *so* big.

It's easy for us to distance ourselves from biblical characters. The stories are familiar, tucked away in an appropriate theological file in our brain. Sometimes they lose their impact because of their very familiarity. We think we know the stories, but perhaps their full impact is waiting for us on a shelf in our souls.

Job had an experience that speaks to every one of us whether we have been touched by a tragedy as deep as his or not. He faced everything that is terrible. He lost his children, his property, his livelihood, and his health. He lost his wife, too. She was still there in body but dead inside. As he sat in a ghastly heap using broken pieces of pottery to scratch his festering wounds, he was subject to the opinions and religious baggage of his "friends." Job's whole story is deeply troubling. All sorts of books and articles have been written about it in an effort to make sense of a heavenly Father who would give the keys of the nursery to a wolf. Isn't that what God did? Satan said, "Let me have him," and God said, "You can't kill him, but you can drive him to the very edge."

We don't know the time span of the story, but what we can't get away from is Job's response at its conclusion. God pulls back the curtain just enough to let Job see as much as a human being could contain of the knowledge of the Almighty. It's the opposite of the Wizard of Oz. This is not a "Pay no attention to the man behind the curtain" moment. This is, "I'm over here. Look if you dare. Look if you can bear it!"

Even as the scabs are crusting on his body, Job cries from the depths of his battered soul, "Surely I spoke of things I did not understand, things too wonderful for me to know. You said, 'Listen now, and I will speak; I will question you, and you shall answer me.' My ears had heard of you but now my eyes have seen you. Therefore I despise myself and repent in dust and ashes" (Job 42:3-6).

The word *repent* used in this text is an interesting one. Job endured more than I can imagine. Why should he repent? He did have his faithless moments, the pounding of his fists on heaven's doors, but no wonder! The Hebrew word here for "repent" can easily be translated as "comfort." He had seen God, and so he was comforted. He now understood that God was his friend, not his enemy or his tormentor. Job changed his mind, and God transformed his life. That is still a mystery to me, but I believe it.

Simone Weil writes in *Gravity and Grace,* "The false god changes suffering into violence. The True God changes violence into suffering." I believe that when we finally see God face to face, all the questions and scars and stones we have carried through life will drop in wonder as we fall on our faces and worship him. I used to say, "When I get to heaven,

I'm going to ask God…" I'm sure you can fill in your own blank. Now I don't think that's what will happen at all. Instead, I'm certain we will fall on our faces and call out in a loud voice: "Worthy is the Lamb, who was slain, to receive power and wealth and wisdom and strength and honor and glory and praise!" (Revelation 5:12). "So it was that to Job," writes Weil, "when once the veil of flesh had been rent by afflictions, the world's stark beauty was revealed."

This world can seem like such a harsh, cruel place, but God is at work here if we will open our eyes to see him and our ears to hear him say, "Peace be with you."

"IT IS WELL WITH MY SOUL"

This beautiful hymn has comforted and strengthened thousands of battered saints. It has whispered peace into unquiet places. It has been sung at funerals and sung as a statement of faith through many dark nights of the human soul.

Peace is more than a feeling of well-being, for surely that was not what Horatio Spafford was experiencing when he wrote those words. They went far deeper than that. He could never have imagined when he put each word on paper how God would use that broken place of worship in his life to be a balm in Gilead to so many through the years.

Horatio Spafford was forty-three years old when he wrote his famous hymn. He was a successful businessman in Chicago. He and his wife had four daughters and had waited for a long time for a baby boy, a son to carry on the family name. When he was born, their lives must have seemed complete. Spafford was a good man who loved God and loved his family. Then the first tragedy struck. Their baby son lived only a few months. Shortly after his death, the Great Chicago Fire of 1871 hit, and Spafford and his family suffered financial disaster. He knew they all needed to get away for a while and recover.

His friend Dwight L. Moody was holding evangelistic crusades in

England that fall, so Spafford decided to take the whole family there. His wife and daughters went ahead on the SS *Ville du Havre*. He planned to follow in a few days. But on the crossing, the ship carrying his family was hit by an iron sailing vessel, and in only twelve minutes it sank into the icy waters of the Atlantic. Two hundred and twenty-six people died that day, including Horatio Spafford's four daughters. His wife lived, and when the survivors were brought ashore in Cardiff, Wales, she sent a weighty two-word cable to her husband: "Saved alone."

He boarded the next ship that was sailing to England. When they reached the place where the ship had gone down, the captain stood beside Horatio and indicated that this was indeed the spot where his daughters lost their lives. "No," Spafford corrected the captain. "This is where their real lives began." He went down to his cabin, picked up a pen, and on ship's stationery wrote the words to the hymn that opens this chapter.

How could he write them? How could he stand looking into the cruel waves that pulled his daughters under their tow and with a broken heart sing such a song of praise? I don't pretend to have all the answers to that mystery. God met him with a well of grace at a watery grave? God poured his love deep into open wounds? It is one thing to say the Lord's Prayer; it is quite another to be held by the Shepherd when you have no strength of your own left.

At the end of a month in a psychiatric hospital, this is the heading I wrote in my journal: *Finger Painting with Picasso.* I felt like a clumsy child starting over in my life. I was acutely aware of my inability to do anything apart from God, and yet I could not deny the divine invitation to join him at the canvas of my life. He saw my sticky fingers and bruised knees and called me to stand beside him. God doesn't need my help, but he loves to work through me. He doesn't need my gifts, but he delights to flow through them. Being broken is a strangely comforting thing; it makes me, with Job, want to repent.

In Walter Percy's book *Love in the Ruins,* the hero of the story is

Dr. Tom More, a psychiatrist haunted by his own private demons of depression. Eventually the darkness is too much for him, and in a table-turning moment he becomes the patient. In that place of shadows, in the valley of tears, he finds a companionship that I understand and celebrate. "I felt so bad that I groaned an Old Testament lamentation, AAAAIEOOOW!" More writes. "To which responded a great silent black man sitting next to me on the blocky couch: 'Ain't it the truth though.' After that I felt better."

How often have you felt like letting out a titanic "AAAAIEOOOW!"? The great aches of the soul don't have words. They are howls so deep that they cross language barriers.

Fyodor Dostoevsky was criticized by reviewers for raising so many questions on suffering in his brilliant book *The Brothers Karamazov,* yet providing so few answers. His response was, "It is not like a child that I believe in Christ and confess him. My hosanna has come through the crucible of doubt."

Peace comes at a price. It came at a price to Christ, and it comes at a price to us as we take his hand in dark places.

It was late on Christmas Day 2000. It was cold and frosty outside but not snowing. We had all eaten more than our fill. Barry and my mom sat by the roaring fire. Mom's head was nodding, and I knew she was taking what she calls "forty winks." Barry was watching a football game, and Christian was looking intently out the window. I came over and stood beside him.

"Can we go outside, Mom?" he asked.

"It's cold, darling," I said.

"I know. But I'd like to go out."

We bundled up in coats and scarves and gloves and walked across the grass that crunched under our feet like potato chips. Christian stopped and stared up at the sky.

"Merry Christmas, Papa," he said. He was quiet for a moment, then he let out a little "AAAAIEOOOW!" It took me by surprise. He took himself by surprise! He did it again a little louder. I joined in. For several moments we howled together. I'm glad we live in the countryside, or someone would have called the police. It sounded as if an entire tribe was being slaughtered. Then we walked home hand in hand. Peace is not the absence of pain, but the presence of God in the midst of it.

PASSING IT ON

Timothy Jones in *Nurturing a Child's Soul* talks about the family as the "forming center" for our children. The home is where stories are told, conversations overheard, reactions observed, prayers said, songs sung, and daily life lived. If we as parents have a deep-seated faith in God and a peace that transcends circumstances, then we will be able to pass that on in "forming" our children. If, on the other hand, we are overwhelmed by fear, if there is disquiet in our hearts and in our relationships, then that will form our children.

One of the greatest legacies my mother passed on to my sister, brother, and me was the fruit of the Spirit, so evident in her life. She was a woman at peace. In her thirties she was a widow with three young children and very little income, but she had absolute confidence in God's ability and willingness to be everything to us that we would ever need. So even though we had very little, we didn't worry. Things were cool with Mom, so things were cool with us!

That's how children are. I see Christian look to Barry or me to see how we are reacting to a distressing situation, and if we are fine, then so is he. If he falls and scrapes his knee or bumps his head, he doesn't make a big fuss if we don't. As he gets older and faces more serious issues, I want to pass on to him a solid faith in the abiding goodness and sovereignty of God in all situations. Some of his dreams will materialize, and some will fall apart, but if God is in control, then all the pieces of the puzzle will ultimately fit together, even the ones with strangely shaped edges that you turn round and round trying to see how they could possibly fit anywhere.

In his Times Square Church Pulpit series, David Wilkerson wrote about receiving the news in December 2000 that his granddaughter, Tiffany, was to have tests to detect a possible brain tumor. He had faced cancer three times before in his immediate family. This was an old foe. "As we all waited to hear Tiffany's lab report," Wilkerson says, "I silently prayed for strength to accept whatever the verdict was. At that moment, it didn't matter to me what the theological meaning of grace was. To me it meant having God's peace."

You wouldn't have to hang around me very long to notice that I love television. I always have. I love movies, too. Barry laughs at the familiar sight of me with headphones on, plugged into my laptop computer, watching a digital videodisc. It's an escape for me, a way to tune out the noise of the airplane or the hotel air conditioning unit that hasn't been serviced since Noah checked out. But as I ask God to give me eyes to see what matters, I am becoming increasingly aware that the popular media is nibbling away at the family. Now, I am not a shrinking violet in a Laura Ashley dress with a big Bible who wants to live on a farm and grow all her own vegetables (not that there would be anything wrong with that, of course!). Neither am I a woman with a chip the size of North Dakota on her shoulder who feels a need to yell loudly to be heard over men. What I am called to be is a woman in relationship with my husband and son, living within the walls of our home at peace with one another and with deep, sacrificial, mutual respect. "Salt is good," Jesus said, "but if it loses its saltiness, how can you make it salty again? Have salt in yourselves, and be at peace with each other" (Mark 9:50).

What does peace look like within the walls of our homes? There are some familiar family names in our popular culture—from Lucy and Ricky Ricardo, to Edith and Archie Bunker, to Marge and Homer

Simpson. The American family as portrayed on television is a twisted picture.

A recent edition of our local, free parenting magazine in Tennessee had an article entitled "Why Dads Matter." I tore it out and put it in a file I keep of articles that are commentaries on our culture. What has happened to our structure that such an article would be included? When did the value of a father become so low that someone had to write and defend it? In our broken world of divorce and blended families, men are often pushed to the sidelines of their children's lives. Randell Turner, vice president of the National Fatherhood Initiative, writes, "As a son watches his father handle difficult situations, everything from an argument with his wife to a bolt that won't come off the car, he learns how men are able or not able to control their anger."

If we as Christian parents don't take seriously the privilege we've been given to live out God's love in front of our children, then the sarcasm, yelling, and screaming of families depicted in the media will likely desensitize them to what life in the Spirit should look like. The result? The Archie Bunkers or Homer Simpsons become the norm.

I mentioned in chapter 2 how Christian watches the way I respond to Barry. He watches how we are together. He sees if what I want at the moment is more important to me than being loving and kind to the people I love. Peace is not some abstract inner calm; it is a way of living. It is a commitment to the Prince of Peace, who took every right he had and laid it down in submission to the God of love.

The challenge for Christian parents, as I see it, is to balance what is good and true in our contemporary culture with the call to live above the cultural norms. Sometimes those who claim no allegiance to Christ seem to live more godly lives than we do. Perhaps our security as believers tends to dull our passion to allow the fruit of the Spirit to be produced in us. If so, that's a tragedy for our children, because the fruit does not fall far from the tree.

I have a favorite poem, written by Rudyard Kipling, on the wall of my office right behind my desk. It has been my favorite since I was a teenager, and I grow to love it more and more. For me it captures the essence of a person at peace as he or she invites God to produce his divine fruit every day.

"IF"

If you can keep your head when all about you
Are losing theirs and blaming it on you,
If you can trust yourself when all men doubt you,
But make allowance for their doubting too;
If you can wait and not be tired by waiting
Or being lied about, don't deal in lies,
Or being hated, don't give way to hating,
And yet don't look too good, nor talk too wise:

If you can dream—and not make dreams your master;
If you can think—and not make thoughts your aim,
If you can meet with Triumph and Disaster
And treat those two impostors just the same;
If you can bear to hear the truth you've spoken
Twisted by knaves to make a trap for fools,
Or watch the things you gave your life to broken,
And stoop and build 'em up with worn-out tools:

If you can make one heap of all your winnings
And risk it on one turn of pitch-and-toss,
And lose, and start again at your beginnings
And never breathe a word about your loss;
If you can force your heart and nerve and sinew
To serve your turn long after they are gone,

And so hold on when there is nothing in you
Except the Will which says to them: "Hold on!"

If you can talk with crowds and keep your virtue,
Or walk with Kings—nor lose the common touch,
If neither foes nor loving friends can hurt you,
If all men count with you, but not too much;
If you can fill the unforgiving minute
With sixty seconds' worth of distance run,
Yours is the Earth and everything that's in it,
And—which is more—you'll be a Man, my son!

There is a fine line between the spirit of the motivational hype that is rampant in our culture and the peace that comes from being totally settled in our boots regarding the love of God. There is no greater assurance to pass on to our children.

I learned a valuable lesson in parenting from my father-in-law, William. One of the things I saw him do often with Christian was to be still, to sit quietly, to rock him, to sing sweet songs and whisper in his ear. I see the same thing with Sean, Christian's nanny. She pulls Christian onto her lap and talks to him, reads to him, and spends quiet time with him.

Our culture is moving at a hectic pace. Children are anxious and driven. Television shows deliver a new image every couple of seconds and are interrupted with fast and furious commercials meant to arouse in children and teenagers a desire for more than they have. The end result is dissatisfaction and disquiet. But we can show our children there is another way to live.

Sometimes at night Barry, Christian, and I sit on the back patio and listen. No one gets to say anything for ten minutes. That's a long time for a four-year-old! But it's amazing what you hear when you're quiet. It's amazing how you can let the stuff of the day go into God's care in the night air. This is a learned behavior. Most every message we get in our culture tells us to do more and to get more. God's Word encourages us to be still and in that stillness to be more.

"Be still, and know that I am God" (Psalm 46:10). A God who abides, holds us on his lap, and whispers into our ear, "Peace be with you."

Joy

Joyful, joyful, we adore Thee,
God of glory, Lord of love;
Hearts unfold like flowers before Thee,
Opening to the sun above.
Melt the clouds of sin and sadness,
Drive the dark of doubt away;
Giver of immortal gladness,
Fill us with the light of day.

Mortals, join the happy chorus
Which the morning stars began;
Father love is reigning o'er us,
Brother love binds man to man.
Ever singing, march we onward,
Victors in the midst of strife,
Joyful music leads us sunward
In the triumph song of life.

—Henry van Dyke, "Joyful, Joyful, We Adore Thee"

≡ JOY ≡

A LOVE OF LIFE

Rejoice in the Lord always. I will say it again: Rejoice! Let your gentleness
be evident to all. The Lord is near. Do not be anxious about anything,
but in everything, by prayer and petition, with thanksgiving,
present your requests to God. And the peace of God...
will guard your hearts and your minds in Christ Jesus.

PHILIPPIANS 4:4-7

All joy (as distinct from mere pleasure, still more amusement)
emphasizes our pilgrim status; always reminds, beckons, awakens desire.
Our best havings are wantings.

C. S. LEWIS

Henry van Dyke was invited to speak to the student body at Williams College in the beautiful Berkshire Mountains of Massachusetts. During his stay he was moved by the splendor of the scenery around him, by the fragrance that filled the air and assaulted his senses. One afternoon after a long walk he wrote the words to "Joyful, Joyful, We Adore Thee." The next morning he presented the hymn to the college president as a gift. The only instruction was that it had to be sung to the music of Beethoven's "Ode to Joy," and it has been sung that way ever since.

What was it about the mountain air, the craggy peaks, the flowers and foliage that would cause such a profound overflow of joy? What did he experience of the presence of God that touched him so deeply that his soul cried out, "Hearts unfold like flowers before Thee"? When he first published the hymn in 1911, he said that it was to be sung by people who "are not afraid that any truth of science will destroy their religion or that any revolution on earth will overthrow the Kingdom of Heaven." He wrote out of a firm, intentional belief that God is in control, that God is good so life is good.

Henry van Dyke wrote in response to the wonder and greatness of God displayed around him, but it is easy to lose that sense of wonder along the way. We can become hardened by disappointments or cynical as we lay down dreams that elude us. That sense of open-eyed, open-hearted wonder is often seen only in small children.

THE UN-BIRTHDAY PARTY

When Christian turned four in December of 2000, we didn't have a birthday party for him. He didn't want one. His papa had just died, and he was too sad. He didn't want a lot of people around the house. As the following summer approached, his nanny, Sean, said to me, "Don't you think it would be fun to have a small party for Christian now? We could have face painting and games. What do you think?"

Well, from that small, innocent idea a monster grew. Barry and I decided it would indeed be great fun and began to plan the big un-birthday celebration. We talked about themes. We went from cowboys and Indians to space aliens and sea monsters. Finally we settled on the idea of a circus. Barry designed the invitations:

Come to the Big Top for an Un-birthday Party with Ringmaster Christian!

I was busy writing at the time, so I asked Barry if he would take the task of booking one of the entertainers from the party section of our local children's magazine.

I said book *one*. I know I said book just *one*. I planned the food, and Barry and Christian drew how they wanted the top of the cake to look. They wanted a clown in each corner and balloons everywhere. I expected about fifteen children, but as replies came in, the number grew to about thirty and a random assortment of adults, too.

"Can I bring my little brother?"

"My cat's depressed. A party will cheer her up."

"My aunt's here from Florida. She loves your books. Can she come…with her friend?"

It was turning into a zoo, not a circus!

A few days before the party, Barry, Christian, and I were sitting on the patio watching the sun do its grand disappearing act of the day. It took a bow and slipped behind the trees across the lake from our house.

"What entertainer did you manage to get?" I asked Barry.

"Oh, I've got it covered," he replied evasively.

"I'm sure you do, honey. I just wondered who'd be coming, that's all."

"They're all coming, Mommy," Christian said with a big grin.

"Very funny," I said.

"No, really! Daddy booked everybody. Isn't that cool?"

I looked at Barry. I looked at Christian. I waited for them to say, "Just kidding!" They didn't. Christian set off in a one-boy conga line across the grass. "I'm going to have a great big party! I'm going to have a great big party!"

I looked at Barry. Barry looked at me. "What on earth have you done?" I asked.

"Well!" he began. "First the elephant arrives."

"Elephant!"

"Oh, not a real one. It's an Astro Jump, a ten-foot jumpy castle elephant," he assured me. "Then the llama, the pony, and the donkey arrive."

"The llama, the pony, and the donkey! Arc we talking jumpy llama and jumpy pony and donkey?" I asked.

"No, real ones."

"A real llama?" I said. "Do you know that they spit and kick?"

"That's okay. We'll keep him outside," he said.

"Oh, that makes me feel much better. Is that it?"

"No, no! Then Laugh-a-Lot arrives."

"Laugh-a-Lot? I don't want to meet anyone with a name like Laugh-a-Lot! Is she a patient from any institution that I might be aware of?" I inquired.

"Hardly!" he said. "She's a clown, a face painter—and she does things with balloons."

"What things?"

"Just things."

"Does she pick up llama poop with her balloons?" I asked.

"No, I'm pretty sure she doesn't do that."

"Is that it now?" I asked hopefully.

"Yes. Except for Safari Greg."

"Safari Greg. Let's see. What could he possibly do?" I mused.

"You might think this part is a little too much," he said.

"I might think *this* part is too much? Oh do tell!" I couldn't wait to hear what Barry thought might be too much.

"Well, Safari Greg has a fifteen-foot Burmese python, some small snakes, a lizard, and a very large iguana," he said quietly.

I sat with that spectacular picture running through my mind for a moment.

"And are they all free the day of the party? No one is otherwise occupied eating small family pets, I hope? I'd hate to leave anyone out," I said with the conviction of a used-car salesman.

"No, they're all available."

"Oh good," I said. I made a mental note that *I* would book *the* entertainer next year.

The big day arrived. By three o'clock our home was a sight to behold. A pony, a donkey, and a llama the size of Cuba were eating our lovely lawn that we had spent months patching until it was green and lush. Now it was an all-you-can-eat buffet for Eeyore and his buddies. Children were running around everywhere. Laugh-a-Lot didn't show up. Apparently she'd had an accident with a balloon, so she sent Ketchup the clown in her place. There was cake on the floor, cake in my hair, and cake on the pony's tail, and several children were feeding large amounts of cake to an increasingly bloated llama. Face paint transformed sweet-faced little children into images of tigers and lions and dragons and bears.

Then the big moment arrived. Safari Greg! As Christian was the guest of honor, he got to be the assistant. I could hear in my mind the letter I would have to write Mom.

Dear Mom,

I am sorry to inform you that a python ate your darling grandson. He did get some cake first though.

Greg started with some of the smaller beasts. He produced a little orange snake.

"Oh, Mom," Christian pined. "Can I have one of those?"

"We'll talk about it later, darling," I said, staring down Barry with a "if you buy him a snake, you're both moving into the Ramada Inn" look.

Then came the big cahoona, the pièce de résistance. Greg produced a fifteen-foot-long yellow-and-white python from its cage. "Christian, do you want to hold the python?" he asked as the snake wrapped itself around Greg's arm.

"Cool!" Christian said.

I watched as my son stood still and let Safari Greg put what looked like the Loch Ness monster in his arms. He beamed from ear to ear. Christian, that is, not, Monty the python.

"Mom, come here. You need to hold this. It's great!" he said.

Just let me say here, between you and me, that I *hate* snakes. I *really* hate snakes. But I looked in my son's eyes, full of pure joy that he wanted to share, and I let them wrap the big beastie around me.

When everyone had gone home and I'd scraped most of the cake and chips off the floor, the three of us sat outside on the grass, being careful to avoid the little gifts left by our equestrian friends.

"This was the best day of my life!" Christian announced. "I got to try everything!"

A LOVE OF LIFE

What a wonderful statement. I pray that my son retains that appreciation for life, for all things new, for a long, long time. I love the fact that he is not ruled by unreasonable fears. I love the fact that he is willing to try anything. I love his imagination. I love his love of life. The privilege and challenge for Barry and me as parents is to encourage all of that while planting seeds in Christian's fertile heart that will produce a harvest rich in spiritual truths that yield deep and lasting joy.

I think of my own life as a young believer. My mother had very little to worry about in terms of my behavior. I wanted to be in God's house. I was part of everything that was going on for Christian young people, but internally I was like a bird trapped in a cage. I carried such a weight of responsibility and guilt around. I was sure that no matter how much I did for God, it wasn't enough, so I tried to do more. I took on responsibility for the happiness of those around me.

One of my best friends decided that being a Christian was far too restricting, so she swung to the opposite extreme. She partied, got drunk, was raped, and never darkened the door of our church again. My friend and I both believed we had only one choice to make. We represented two extremes produced by our unique perspectives of what it meant to belong to God.

Me: I want to serve God, so I have a list of rules to keep. If I make a mistake, God won't love me anymore. I have this one lifetime to impress God.

She: I want to enjoy my life, spread my wings, experiment. I can't do that and love God, so I'll walk away from him. I'm not sure what lies beyond the now, so I have to find what I feel I need right now.

The problems with both extremes are obvious. The first perspective views life as a test, placing the emphasis on our performance. The second has no view of life or joy beyond this earth.

The challenge for us as parents is to bring all of life together under the safe shelter of the boundless love of God, to demonstrate by example a love so big that our children will be anchored to God's heart. A secure child knows that he can kick up his heels a little and still be welcome at the dinner table. So too with our relationship with Abba, our heavenly Father.

In his book *Abba Father,* Brennan Manning relates the story of Edward Farrel, a priest from Detroit who took a vacation in Ireland. One morning he was enjoying an early morning walk around Lake Kilarney with his Uncle Seamus. They stopped for a moment to watch the sun rise across the water.

Suddenly the uncle turned and went skipping down the road. He was radiant, beaming, smiling from ear to ear. His nephew said, "Uncle Seamus, you look really happy."

"I am lad."

"Want to tell me why?"

His eighty-year-old uncle replied, "Yes, you see my Abba is very fond of me."

Do you feel that joy-producing love when you look at a summer sky, decorated with puffy white clouds? When you feel the rain on your face or the wind at your back, do you hear the Father's love song? *I love you. I love you. I love you.*

It's almost impossible to love life if you don't feel loved. I want Christian to know that he is eternally loved by a God who cannot change his mind. God loves him, and there's nothing he can do about it! I pray that the magnificence of that perfect love will propel him into God's arms, where he will be secure at the deepest core of his being.

ANCHORED TO THE HEART OF GOD

Happiness is dependent on circumstances. Joy is not. Happiness is fleeting, but joy is eternal. It's hard to teach that to children. You have to model it. I saw it as I grew up, watching my mother's life. I saw her responses to disappointments and financial struggle. What I took away from all those scattered impressions of youth was a firm conviction that God is in control, God is good, we are never alone, and we are always loved. I saw joy in action. Even in times of loss there was an anchor for my mom and for us that held us steady during the storm. What a heritage!

I remember flying home from the south of France, where I was working with Youth for Christ, to attend my maternal grandmother's funeral. I was devastated at the news that she was gone. As I sat on the plane, I remembered Sunday mornings as a child, sitting beside her in church, cozying up to her fur coat, and smelling the fragrance that was Nana to me. I thought of Saturday mornings spent running errands for her or sitting in her little kitchen sharing an ice cream float. I could remember the smell of that kitchen, always some fresh scones or shortbread just coming out of the oven. I thought of Christmas mornings, waiting for Nana to get her dressing gown on so we could all creep downstairs together to see if Santa had come. I thought of her smile and her rosy red cheeks, and tears ran in rivers down my face. This was my mom's mom, and I knew she would miss her so much. They were more than mother and daughter. They were friends who had walked through the fire together, through my grandfather's Alzheimer's and my father's death, and her absence would be deeply felt.

I don't remember much about the funeral service that day, but I remember my mom's expression as we stood at the cemetery in the bitter cold of a Scottish afternoon. I saw the tears of sadness and the pain of saying good-bye in my mother's eyes. But there was also an inner strength there that I certainty didn't have at that time. "This good-bye is not forever," my mom said. "This is what we are living for. Nana is home free now."

> Ever singing, march we onward,
> Victors in the midst of strife,
> Joyful music leads us sunward
> In the triumph song of life.

My mother's confidence and strength had a deep impact on me as a young woman. Although I didn't know it then, there were many moments when my mother was teaching me some of the most important lessons of life. These were not moments found in reading books or even in face-to-face talks but in observing my mom's faith in action. As I walked beside her, I saw joy.

If all we pass on to our children is a "right" to be happy, then we have missed the mark. Happiness is not nearly enough. Happiness is something we seek and plan for; it is outside ourselves. But joy is internal and eternal. Blaise Pascal wrote in *Pensées*, "Since we are always planning how we are going to be happy, it is inevitable that we never are." Christian joy declares that God is in control of all of life, cares about all of life, and longs to fill all of our lives with his fragrance.

AN ETERNAL PERSPECTIVE

True joy comes from a vision of life that lies beyond this life. If this life is all we have, then we are compelled to squeeze every ounce of pleasure out of whatever we perceive will make us happy. We think,

If only I were married, I'd be happy.
If I only had a child, I'd be happy.
If only I could get that career break I deserve, I'd be happy.
If only I were thinner, taller, smarter…

The list is as endless as human desire. But even if we get those things we perceive will fill the void, we are left with the emptiness of realizing that what we are longing for at the core of our beings is not what we thought we were longing for. As C. S. Lewis wrote, "What does not satisfy when we find it was not the thing we were desiring."

When I was in my twenties, I was invited to tour South Africa with British pop legend Cliff Richard. He had produced two albums for me, and we had become friends. Cliff is a unique performer who has remained at the top of the charts in most of the world for almost forty years. He has sold more singles than the Beatles, the Rolling Stones, and the Who put together. He is also a very committed follower of Christ.

A few days into the tour, on a day off, we were invited to the country estate of a wealthy, influential South African businessman. The party was a who's who of the rich and famous. There were movie stars, models, the reigning Miss Universe, and enough alcohol to drown a boatload of sailors. I told Cliff that I felt very uncomfortable there.

"Just wait awhile, Sheila, and let's see what God will do. This is as much a mission field as any we could encounter on tour."

As the day progressed and the sun began to set over the ocean, I noticed that people were beginning to gather around us. They wanted to talk to Cliff. They asked him questions about his relationship with God, about his lifestyle, about fear and longing, about hope and unfulfilled dreams. It was one of the most honest and vulnerable dialogues I have ever been privileged to be a part of. As we were driving back to the hotel that night, I told Cliff how surprised I was at the tangible yearning, even despair, often just beneath the surface of people our culture views as the favored few.

"Think about it, Sheila," he said. "So many people think, 'If I were thinner or richer or more gifted, I would be happy. If I could just get that break, everything would change.' But what happens if you get to climb to the very top of the ladder, open the golden box, and find out that it's empty? Where do you turn then?"

As I reflect now on that evening, I remember a lot of laughter and little joy.

The world has nothing enduring to offer that fills the need we all have for love. True joy doesn't come with more "stuff" but from a deep assurance of the relentless love of God.

THE GREATEST JOY

We all long for good things for our children, but nothing compares to a personal relationship with Christ. Before Christian was born, his father and grandparents and I began to pray for his salvation. There is no greater privilege or joy for a parent than to be part of anchoring one's child to the heart of God.

I was talking to my mom one day recently, getting an update on the family. "How's Aunt Mary?" I asked, inquiring about our family matriarch.

"She's holding her own," Mom replied. "You know Aunt Mary!"

I certainly do. She is fiercely independent and wonderfully kind. She is a link to a past in Scotland where people lived off the land, chopped all their own firewood, and scrubbed their laundry clean on a washboard.

"There's great news about John," Mom said, referring to my sister's sixteen-year-old son.

"What's that?" I asked excitedly. I have always been very fond of my nephew.

"I can't tell you," she replied.

"What do you mean you can't tell me?" I asked indignantly.

"He wants to tell you himself."

"Well, why did you tell me anything then?" I asked. "I'll be up all night wondering. Please tell me he's not getting married," I said.

"I said it was good news," Mom replied.

I called my sister's number and asked to speak to John. "Oh, he's out," Frances said.

"I hear there's some good news," I said, probing.

"Wonderful news!" she replied.

"Wonderful! We've crossed into wonderful. Can you tell me what we're talking about?"

"He wants to tell you himself. It means a lot to him," she replied.

Finally, after a few misses across the Atlantic, I touched base with my nephew. "So how are you?" I asked.

"I've never been better in my whole life," he assured me with the passionate resonance of a captivated teenager.

"Tell me about it," I urged.

He told me the story of a recent mission trip to England that he'd been part of with some young people at church. "One night, Aunt Sheila," he said, "I felt as if God was speaking to me, right to me! I've never felt anything like it in my life, but I prayed and asked Jesus to come into my heart."

I couldn't even respond. Tears were pouring down my cheeks. As a family we had been praying for my nephews for some time. John has been in church since he was a baby but had never taken that step of making his relationship with Christ personal and passionate.

"I want to go to Bible college and serve God the rest of my life," he said.

"Wow! What happened to playing soccer for Scotland?" I asked.

"This would be better," he answered.

There was rejoicing in heaven over the salvation of John Burns. There was rejoicing on the west coast of Scotland over the salvation of John Burns. And there was rejoicing ten miles south of Nashville, too!

There is no greater joy in life than when our children make that decision to love and serve God for themselves. Plumbing the depths of a relationship with Christ is what Sadhu Sundar Singh calls "a hidden and inexhaustible mine." Sadhu has been called the Saint Paul of India. He was a very devout child raised in the Sikh religion. His mother died when he was a teenager, and his grief drove him to rail at God, even publicly burning the Bibles of the Christian missionaries in the area. His desperation became so intense that he decided to plan his own death. He gave God three days to show up and prove that he was real. If he failed to do so, Sadhu intended to end his life and his miserable spiritual quest on the railroad tracks near his home.

On the third day he had a vision of the risen Christ that transformed his life. Sadhu went on to become one of the most remarkable missionaries of the twentieth century. He wrote, "Real joy and peace do not depend on power, kingly wealth, or other material possessions. If this were so, all people of wealth in the world would be happy and contented, and princes like Buddha, Mahavira, and Bhartari would not have renounced their kingdom. But this real and permanent joy is found only in the Kingdom of God, which is established in the heart when we are born again."

Jesus declared clearly, "I tell you the truth, no one can see the kingdom of God unless he is born again" (John 3:3). We can pray for our children. We can look for ways to share with them the joy of our own relationship with Christ. We can invite godly, fun people to our home, knowing the potency of the fragrance of Christ that flows from those who love him. But ultimately our greatest privilege is to anchor them to the heart of God by making his love irresistible as we live it out before them day by day.

I consciously point Christian's attention back toward God in the dailiness of walking in his two shoes every day. I don't want him to grow up thinking that God exists within the four walls of a church but rather that he permeates all of life and cares about all of life. So often we miss that in our culture.

I think of the movie *Chariots of Fire* and that wonderful declaration of athlete Eric Liddell: "When I run, I feel his pleasure." Many people are miserable in life because they are living someone else's dream for their life rather than finding out what they are good at and doing it with a heart full of gratitude to God. Others are miserable because they believe the lie that only those in so-called "ministry" are doing anything of eternal value.

I had a conversation with a woman at a conference that made me very sad. She said, "I want to do something with my life. I want to do something worthwhile like you."

"What do you do at the moment?" I asked.

"Well, I don't have a job at the moment. I have four children."

"Wow! Sounds like a job to me!" I said.

"I mean I want to do something for God," she answered.

"I can't think of anything that God would care more about than loving and treasuring four little lives," I persisted. "How old are they?" I asked. She told me that her children were all under ten.

"That would seem like a pretty worthwhile, full-time 'ministry' to me," I said.

"But I want to do something important," she continued, frustrated that I wasn't getting her point.

We talked for some time but parted on other sides of the planet. I thought about those children. I wondered in what ways they pick up messages from their mom that what she is engaged in with them is not "enough." I thought about her and prayed for her. What was she told at some point in her life to make her believe that her value in life was dependent on the culture's values?

GETTING IT

I took my car in to be serviced recently because I was having a problem with the automatic seat adjustment on the driver's side. I told the service manager what my problem was. He said, "Page forty-two of your car manual."

"Wow! You didn't miss a beat. How did you know that without looking it up?" I asked.

"It's my job to know that. This is my life."

If you'll forgive the somewhat corny analogy, I thought about how often I try to "fix my life" without referring to the manual. Everything that you and I need to know as we look through a glass darkly is spelled out in God's Word. If we are to have joy in life, we must "get" the fact that God has stamped his love on every page of our lives. God *is* our life.

I began this chapter with Christian's outrageous joy at his un-birthday party, but not all days end on that note. In the summer of 2001 we signed him up for soccer camp at the YMCA. This was his first experience of teamwork. On the last evening of the week-long camp, Coach Charlie divided the ten four-year-olds into two teams. Barry and I were the goal posts! Christian's team had the ball, and they were heading toward the goal. He had dribbled it most of the way down the field when he stumbled and lost control of the ball. One of his teammates was right behind him and continued down the field and scored a goal. The team was ecstatic. Everyone, that is, apart from Christian. He started to cry and refused to go back on the field. I told him in no uncertain terms to get back on the field and congratulate his teammate who had scored the winning goal. He was mad at me and did what I told him only through clenched teeth. That night we had a talk.

"When you are part of a team, darling, if someone in your team wins, you win," I said.

"But I wanted to score!" he moaned.

"I understand that. You did a great job getting the ball as far as you did, and your teammate did a great job finishing up the play. Life is not all about your getting your own way or even about your winning; it's about your doing your very best and loving life in the process."

I can tell I'll be preaching this one for a long time. Christian is not yet convinced. But what is joy? It's not the self-serving pursuit of happiness that our sinful hearts would choose again and again; it's the daily taking up of our cross in Jesus' name and worshiping God in all the moments of our days. It's offering all of life to him, knowing that in the dark moments when life does not go as we planned, God is here, God is good, and God loves us.

Vision

Be Thou my Vision, O Lord of my heart;
Nought be all else to me, save that Thou art—
Thou my best thought, by day or by night,
Waking or sleeping, Thy presence my light.

Riches I heed not, nor man's empty praise,
Thou mine inheritance, now and always:
Thou and Thou only, first in my heart,
High King of heaven, my Treasure Thou art.

High King of heaven, my victory won,
May I reach heaven's joys, O bright heaven's Sun!
Heart of my own heart, whatever befall,
Still be my Vision, O Ruler of all.

—Ancient Irish hymn, "Be Thou My Vision"

⚌ VISION ⚌

LOVE ON FIRE

My soul is consumed with longing for your laws at all times.

PSALM 119:20

Jesus Christ and Saint Paul have much oftener used this method of the heart,
which is that of love, than that of the understanding.
Because their principle purpose was not so much to inform as to inflame.

BLAISE PASCAL·

Do everything to make everyman eternally responsible for every hour he lives,
even for the least thing he undertakes, for this is Christianity.

SØREN KIERKEGAARD

I was recently introduced to the writings of Blaise Pascal, a brilliant mathematician who is regarded as the father of the modern computer. He was born in Clermont in central France in 1623. When he was seven years old, the king of France promoted his father to the position of Royal Commissioner in Charge of Taxes for Normandy, so the family moved to Paris and into a life of affluence and free-thinking liberalism.

When Blaise was twenty-four, he made a commitment to follow Christ, but he struggled between his devotion to God and his love of fast living and the whirlwind of the Parisian lifestyle. Then he had a radical encounter with Christ that changed the remainder of his life. On the evening of 23 November 1654, having just escaped harm in a carriage accident, he was caught up with God in what he described as an ecstatic experience that lasted for over two hours. The only word he could find to describe the encounter was "fire." When he "came to himself," he wrote down every impression he could remember. The following is an excerpt.

> God of Abraham, God of Isaac, God of Jacob, not of
>   philosophers and scholars.
> Certitude, heartfelt joy, peace.
> God of Jesus Christ.
> "My God and your God."
> "Your God shall be my God."
> The world forgotten, everything except God.
> Joy, joy, joy, tears of joy.
> Complete and sweet renunciation
> Total submission to Jesus Christ.
> I will not neglect your Word.
> Amen.

When Pascal died eight years later, the text in full was found on a piece of parchment sewn inside his jacket. He had moved it from jacket to jacket over the years. The words by which he tried to capture his fiery encounter with the living Christ had been literally next to his heart ever since that night.

The reason I draw attention to this remarkable man in the context of living out the love of God before our children is that I am hungry to have a heart on fire. I don't want more knowledge about God; I want to know him in a way that would set my heart ablaze. I don't want to simply talk about the love of God; I want to be consumed by it. I have been a Christian for more than thirty years. I have swung between extremes, from believing it's up to me to impress God to a complacency that borders on lethargy. If there is nothing I can do to win God's freely offered favor, why try?

Now, at forty-five, I realize that the only thing in this life worth pursuing with all that is within me is the greatest romance offered to any man, woman, or child: a passionate love affair with God. This is what I want for my son. I hope Christian makes good choices in life and finds a satisfying and noble career, but much more than that I pray that he will hear the call of God in his heart and that his passion will be set on things eternal. I want him to live his life here on earth with vision and purpose, responding to the call of Christ: "Come, follow me!" (Matthew 4:19). Nothing else really matters or satisfies.

In *Wild at Heart,* author John Eldridge says of the church, "Men are bored and women are tired." Why are men bored? Perhaps because we have dumbed-down the call of God, removing the exhortation for courage and a radical love. Men need what Søren Kierkegaard described as "an idea for which I can live and die." The alternative is what Henry David Thoreau called a life "of quiet desperation."

Why are women tired? Perhaps because we are running around trying to do everything in our homes and our churches and have lost the heart of Mary of Bethany, who chose the better path and sat at Jesus' feet while Martha self-combusted. All I am sure of is that without a sense of divine calling, we are internally lost. What we need is a vision from God, a sense of purpose, an understanding of the call of God on our lives, and the joy that comes from remaining true to that call.

Vision is critical for life. Without it we perish. In his book *The Seven Pillars of Wisdom,* T. E. Lawrence, better known as Lawrence of Arabia, wrote, "All men dream: but not equally. Those who dream by night in the dusty recesses of their minds wake in the day to find it was vanity: but the dreamers of the day are dangerous men, for they may act their dreams with open eyes, to make it possible. This I did."

There is a difference between arrogance and nobility. Arrogance raises itself against God, but nobility bows humbly before God and accepts life as a divine quest with all its joys and sorrows, wins and losses.

THE CALL

One of the best books I have ever read is *The Call* by Os Guinness. In the early spring of 2001, Os spent a couple of days with the six Women of Faith speakers and a few other members of our team. The intent was to encourage and challenge us to think outside our narrow paradigms as we seek to communicate the love of God to women in all walks of life and places of faith or fear. Os did far more. He gave an amazing overview of Christian history that seemed to go from the ascension of Christ to last Tuesday. In his brilliance he exhibits a tender, winsome love for God, which has left an indelible mark on my soul. After being with him, I wanted to read some of his books and began with *The Call.* I highly recommend this book to anyone longing for a clear vision of our purpose here on earth.

I look at the resources that are available to us parents as we attempt to shepherd our children's hearts toward God. Having been raised in the church, I am a committed believer in Sunday school, Vacation Bible School, and backyard Bible clubs; but there has to be more. A child can grow up with a mind full of memorized Scripture verses and little sense of the bigger picture of the adventure of following Christ.

Perhaps the concept of "full-time Christian service" I mentioned in the previous chapter has played a role in removing the wonder of worshiping God in every moment, in everything we do. Os Guinness addresses this in his book, explaining the split that occurred early in the fourth century when Christian life was divided into two distinct parts: the perfect and the permitted. This split can be traced back to Eusebius.

Eusebius, Bishop of Caesarea, is regarded as the principal historian of the early church. His prolific writings cover much of the birth of the church to the conversion of Emperor Constantine in A.D. 312. In his work *Demonstration of the Gospel,* Eusebius introduced a segregation of sacred and secular life that led to an elitist view of Christian service. By his standard only a few are called to serve God; the rest of us muddle on in mundane work that has nothing spiritual to offer. If you are a priest or church worker, you have the privilege of living the "perfect" life. If you are a mom or a CEO, you are relegated to the "permitted" life.

Think about how this must have affected believers in Eusebius's time. If you were not called to serve in church work, then you had little to offer God. And perhaps worse, you'd be left dragging through your days without a sense of purpose. But don't you see the same thinking rampant in the church today? We look at our pastors, missionaries— anyone in so-called full-time Christian service—as those who have God's special favor. Everyone else just muddles through. No wonder men are bored and women are tired! We were made by God to live with fiery passion and purpose, and without that we flounder.

I think back to the celebrities at the party I attended with Cliff Richard, and I see this point reinforced. It's not enough to be good at something. It's not enough to have your face pasted on every magazine on the rack. It's not enough to have everyone else envy your life if inside you have no sense of peace and purpose. That is our challenge and privilege as believers and as parents: to discover our divine call and to model that purposeful life to our children.

I wrestled for years to discover the purpose of my life. For too long it was a job, something I did rather than who I am in Christ. I am settled now that the purpose of my life is to receive the huge love of God and allow him to love others through me. That means if Women of Faith or Children of Faith ends, if I can no longer write or sing or make a living doing the things I love, my identity in Christ is secure. That is a settled thing. I lost everything once, and it was a liberating, soul-stretching experience. When you face your worst fears and find God present in them, life takes on a quiet joy.

Os Guinness recalls a quote from an early draft of Dostoevsky's *The Brothers Karamazov*. The Inquisitor gives a chilling account of what happens to a human soul when it doubts its purpose: "For the secret of man's being is not only to live...but to live for something definite. Without a firm notion of what he is living for, man will not accept life and will destroy himself rather than remain on earth."

Does that sound familiar? Pick up a newspaper or turn on the television, and Dostoevsky's nightmare stares right back. I have a dear friend whose fourteen-year-old boy has attempted to take his life. There is no father in the picture; instead, the mother has had a couple of uninspiring boyfriends. There have been a few geographic moves, and in his soul this boy feels anchorless. Without a sense of purpose, he finds his life not worth living.

Jesus said to his disciples, "If anyone would come after me, he must deny himself and take up his cross and follow me. For whoever wants to save his life will lose it, but whoever loses his life for me will find it. What good will it be for a man if he gains the whole world, yet forfeits his soul?" (Mathew 16:24-26). Far more than a "Turn left at the next intersection," the call to follow Christ is to live as he lived, love as he loved, and experience the vision and passion he experienced.

I believe it is possible for every believer to experience a life of passion and profound meaning, regardless of circumstances, race, gifts, or length of days. Why, then, are so many of us who love God dissatisfied with our lives?

On my desk at the moment is a letter from Dr. Richard Mouw, president of Fuller Seminary in Pasadena, California. I was a student at Fuller, and Barry worked on staff, so we get updates every now and then regarding life on campus. This letter, however, was more personal, reflecting on Dr. Mouw's past thirty years in Christian education. He began by talking about what he had thought God wanted him to do when he was a little boy. "In those services of my childhood we sang hymns that emphasized total surrender to the will of God: 'If by a still small voice he calls to paths that I do not know, I'll answer, "Dear Lord, with my hand in Thine, I'll go where you want me to go." '"

I smiled as I read on. Like me, he had felt that to please God he would need to be a missionary in a tropical rain forest somewhere, leading people to Christ. What he really loved, however, was books. He loved to read, to study, to write, and to pass on his thoughts. From time to time as he pursued his career in academia, he was plagued with little stabs of guilt, wondering if he had chosen the easy path rather than the one of true sacrifice. He loved what he was doing so much. Could this be God's will?

In his letter it was clear that he had come to embrace the liberating news that the enjoyable path isn't by nature the wrong one. I wholeheartedly concur. My sister is a teacher. She loves it, and she is a great teacher. I, on the other hand, would rather stick my leg in a blender than teach ten-year-olds. My brother is an architect. He has a senior position with the largest private firm in England. His designs have fantastic detail and style, whereas I can't draw a straight line. We all came from the same mother and father, lived in the same home, and turned out gloriously different. We were taught by my mother to embrace and celebrate those differences. As I think back on my childhood, I think of my home as being as much of a sanctuary as our church was. I want that for Christian, too. As a family we include God in our whole lives, not just when we are on the road serving God and people through our various ministries. Real life is lived out on Monday mornings and Tuesday evenings as much as, if not more than, on our Friday nights or Sunday mornings.

And that's the whole point for each of us. As we raise our children, God's love and presence in all the moments of our lives is the whole point. There is no greater privilege than passing on a passion that comes from a proper vision of being in relationship with God.

HOLY ORDERS

Eugene Peterson, translator of the popular Bible *The Message,* grew up in a small town in Montana. He recollects his childhood as being lived in two holy places: the small village church and his father's butcher shop. In *Leap over a Wall* Peterson writes, "Work and worship were aspects of one world. The world of work was a holy place for me." Every year his mother made a new butcher's apron for him to accommodate that year's growth. When he was a young man, Eugene assumed it was of the same cut and design as the garment Hannah made for her son, Samuel, as he trained alongside Eli the priest. "My father was a priest in our butcher shop, and I was with him. Our butcher shop was a place of blessing."

What a gift to be raised in an atmosphere where all of life is holy and everything matters. What a gift to know that the love of God assures we can come as we are and be welcomed into the presence of God in all the moments of our lives. Peterson writes that twenty-five years later, as a pastor, he's well aware of the way people change when they enter a church. They leave half of their vocabulary outside, they change the tone in their voices, and they bring only part of themselves to God. "I'm still engaged in that work," he writes, "saying and show-ing—insisting!—that the world of work is the primary context for spir-ituality, for experiencing God, for obeying Jesus, for receiving the Spirit. And I'm not finding it any easier."

Every Christian takes holy orders. That is Eugene Peterson's convic-tion. That is Os Guinness's conviction. It was Paul's conviction too. "Therefore, I urge you, brothers, in view of God's mercy, to offer your bodies as living sacrifices, holy and pleasing to God—this is your spirit-ual act of worship. Do not conform any longer to the pattern of this world, but be transformed by the renewing of your mind. Then you will be able to test and approve what God's will is—his good, pleasing and perfect will" (Romans 12:1-2).

As Sir Winston Churchill said in a speech in Parliament in 1941, "Nothing is more dangerous than to live in the temperamental atmosphere of a Gallup Poll, always feeling one's pulse and taking one's temperature." He referred to the inconsistencies and treachery of the political world, but the warning holds true in the church. We can be busy doing things for God and yet be far away from him in our hearts. We can win the approval of those around us and yet have no vision or passion for a life lived for God alone. But if all of life is sacred and we live before an audience of one, then there is no casual, unimportant moment. Søren Kierkegaard's words ring true: "Do everything to make everyman eternally responsible for every hour he lives, even for the least thing he undertakes, for this is Christianity."

I ask myself how keeping that focus clear would change my life and choices. How would it change the lives of those around me? How would it change the life of my son?

SPLENDOR IN THE ORDINARY

I heard a fascinating story from Os Guinness concerning his ancestry. It touched me deeply because it is a story from my homeland but also because it exquisitely illustrates the joy and passion of a life lived for God. Os's great-great-grandmother was named Jane Lucretia D'Esterre. She was widowed at eighteen and left with two small children. In her despair she decided to end her life in the cold, murky waters of a Scottish river. But as she gazed with sorrow into the dark depths, she looked up and saw a young plowman at work. He was plowing his fields meticulously and whistling hymns as he went about his work. Something about this man's devotion to the task at hand and the manner in which he went about it arrested her attention. She turned from the river with a renewed commitment to life. Not long after that she became a believer and a woman of prayer. From that turning back came a whole new line of believers and the gift of Os Guinness to our culture as an apologist for the church to the world and an interpreter of the world to the church.

What did Jane Lucretia see? She saw the splendor of the ordinary. God in the mundane. God in everything.

This kind of vision leaves no place for envy. Calling and envy are diametrically opposed. The temptation when we raise boys, in particular, is to pit them against one another. We hold up competition as the making of a man. I strongly disagree. Team sports are wonderful. They teach us that we are not the point. They teach us that as I help you, I am helped. But too often competition becomes a way of life.

"I am good at this, but are you better?"

"I paint well, but do you paint better?"

"I love to play golf, but I'm not playing with him because he thinks he is better."

None of this has a place in the heart of the one who is called by God and who lives his or her life doing everything he can to honor God with what he has. Jesus' parables made that clear.

In a parable recorded in Matthew 25:14-30, Jesus told the story of a wealthy businessman about to depart on a long journey who decided to share some of his property with three of his servants. In contemporary terms, the businessman gave the first servant five thousand dollars, the next two thousand dollars, and the last one a thousand dollars. The man who had been given five thousand dollars bought a small, run-down feed store, refurbished it, and sold it for ten thousand dollars. The employee with two thousand dollars invested in the stock exchange and doubled his investment. The man with one thousand dollars put the cash in a shoebox under his bed. "You can't trust banks these days," he said to his wife over a sparse supper.

Sometime later the businessman returned from his overseas trip and called his employees into his office to find out what they had done with the money. The first man told him how he had purchased the rundown store, renovated it, and sold it for double the money. His employer was very impressed and instantly promoted him. He was also very pleased with the second man and upped his salary too. The third man crawled like a Palestinian Uriah Heep up to his master's desk and said, "Well, you see, you're a tough man to figure out. I mean, you're brilliant, of course, but for those of us who are not quite as brilliant as your noble self, what are we to do? I had no desire to waste your hard-earned money, so here it is!" He pushed an old shoebox into his master's rapidly reddening face.

The businessman was furious. He took the thousand dollars and gave it to the visionary man who'd made ten thousand dollars out of five thousand. "You at least could have put it in the bank, and I'd have made interest on it," the employer said to Uriah. "My thousand dollars is worth less today than when I gave it to you! Whoever wisely uses what he's given without trying to second-guess his master will be given more, but the one who does nothing with what he's been given, even what he has been given will be taken away."

When we have a clear vision of our purpose in life, then we are free from the treadmill of trying to be like everyone else, and we can live with confidence and joy. Think again of Mozart and Salieri. If Salieri had taken the two talents that God gave him and used them instead of being consumed by the five talents that God gave Mozart, how different his life would have been! This is our privilege as parents, to help our children rejoice over what is true about them rather than mourn what they perceive to be absent.

In the introduction to this book, I talked about common threads in families whose children grew up understanding the love of God. What I found was that those children who were raised by parents who were truly in love with Christ—those who treasured their friendship with God above anything else—were more easily drawn to the heart of God. It wasn't that rules and discipline were absent, but they were not the point. They were the framing of the stage, not the central play itself. The real point was "God is beautiful. You are beautiful. God loves you in your good days and your bad days. There is nothing in this world that could make him stop loving you. God's love is so big that it will never fade away."

The temptation in our crazy culture is for Christian parents to tighten up on all the rules, hoping the walls they build up will lead their children to God. That does not seem to work. In fact, it often seems to have the opposite effect. As G. K. Chesterton wrote, "If there is one thing worse than the modern weakening of major morals, it is the modern strengthening of minor morals."

Musical artist CeCe Winans sings an amazing song, "Alabaster Box." It tells the story of Mary Magdalene making her way through the crowd to break open her box of costly perfume and pour it on Jesus' feet. In the song she asks the crowd not to be angry. She knows they don't understand the gratitude that has compelled her to this act of worship because they weren't there on the night when Jesus saved her. They couldn't possibly comprehend the cost of the oil in her alabaster box.

That is the bottom line of a book like this. The whole point is that until we grasp the enormity of the love of God, we are just going through the motions; but when we begin to grasp how much we are loved, we are transformed, and so is everything around us. We are like the man whom Jesus told to go a second time and wash his eyes. Suddenly he could see everything around him as he had never seen before. Nothing was ordinary. Everything was splendid!

A PARENT'S GREATEST PRIVILEGE

One of the greatest privileges we have as parents is to teach our children that our lives are a continuous journey. We don't know every step, but we know where we are ultimately headed. We know we will never feel quite at home here on earth, so we don't fight the restlessness but use it to draw us closer to the heart of God. We don't make all our choices based on today or even tomorrow but on eternity, because we are people who live for a life beyond this one. In our sorrows we are not as those with no hope, because even our sorrows will be used by God to mold us into his perfect image. We do not strive to be better than anyone else but to serve, to cheer when another wins, for our very cheering is an act of worship. We get up on dreary days, when dreams seem distant and no other human being seems to understand, and live that day passionately, intentionally, because there is One who never slumbers or sleeps but sees everything.

By God's grace we live with a heart ablaze. We live in a way that makes no sense apart from the existence and fiery love of God. In the words of Reinhold Niebuhr, "Nothing we do, however virtuous, can be accomplished alone; therefore, we are saved by love."

What, then, shall we say in response to this? If God is for us, who can be against us? He who did not spare his own Son, but gave him up for us all—how will he not also, along with him, graciously give us all things? Who will bring any charge against those whom God has chosen? It is God who justifies. Who is he that condemns? Christ Jesus, who died—more than that, who was raised to life—is at the right hand of God and is also interceding for us. Who shall separate us from the love of Christ? Shall trouble or hardship or persecution or famine or nakedness or danger or sword? As it is written:

"For your sake we face death all day long;
     we are considered as sheep to be slaughtered."

No, in all these things we are more than conquerors through him who loved us. (Romans 8:31-37)

Amen. Amen. Amen.

ABOUT THE AUTHOR

Sheila Walsh is a powerful Christian communicator who is a unique combination of singer, songwriter, author, speaker, and television talk-show host. She is a featured speaker at the nationwide Women of Faith conferences and creator and host of the national Children of Faith conferences. Former co-host of *The 700 Club* and host of her own show, *Heart to Heart with Sheila Walsh,* she is also the author of several books, including *Honestly* and *Living Fearlessly.* She recently released her latest CD, *Hymns and Worship.* Learn more about her at Sheilawalsh.com.